What people are saying about *Integrity Matters*:

"As a consequence of the plethora of business scandals, there seems to be a great deal of concern about corporate governance. ...*Integrity Matters* clearly shows a need both for businesses and governments to measure how stakeholders view an organization's 'integrity-driven' practices and what that means for our future well-being. Our society in the early 21st century needs people and guidance that are 'on the side of right.' We need to restore the sense of trust in our business and government leaders that we once had...."
> — ALVIN ACHENBAUM, Chairman; PETER B. BOGDA, President;
> Achenbaum Bogda Associates, New York, New York

"Well-written and easy to understand, *Integrity Matters* should be read and acted upon by everyone in an organization."
> — NANCY ALBERTINI, Managing Partner, Inveraray Partners LLC, Dallas, Texas

"Employers, employees, parents, children, leaders of all kinds and of all ages should read this book. *Integrity Matters* is a no-frills, no-nonsense primer on what may well be the next real revolution in business, government and society in general....The great institutions and leaders of the future will have ethics as their hallmark."
> — JAMES H. AUSTGEN, retired senior executive, Lake Barrington, Illinois

"Not since the Great Depression have so many people lost faith in the basic honesty of business leadership in America. ...*Integrity Matters* offers an impressive and practical prescription for better leadership and, in the long run, a better society."
> — E. WILLIAM BARNETT, Managing Partner (retired), Baker Botts LLP,
> Houston, Texas

"This book is a catalyst for American business to assess their ethical practices. This process will confirm high standards or cause necessary action to transform companies to high integrity and superior profits."
> — PAUL BASZUCKI, Chairman, Norstan Inc., Minnetonka, Minnesota

"*Integrity Matters* is a relevant, tangible reference that I will return to again and again."
> — GARM BEALL, Webspace Designs, Woodland Hills, California

"Your prosperity in life is dependent upon your integrity. Jim Bracher has some exceptional insights into the importance of integrity in one's life, both personally and professionally."
> — PETER BURWASH, Founder, Peter Burwash International, The Woodlands, Texas

"There is a real sense of urgency in the message contained within this book, and it behooves everyone who is concerned about the future of the free marketplace to read, study and think about the future of business."
> — C. JAMES CARR, President and Chief Executive Officer, Produce Reporter Co.,
> Blue Book Services, Carol Stream, Illinois

"As an entrepreneur, I've invested capital, time and credibility in over 10 companies ... the difference between success and failure in these new businesses is leadership and integrity. Company management needs to read this book ... and understand that integrity does matter."
> — KENNETH J. CAVALLARO, President, Riverview Partners, Inc.,
> West Newbury, Massachusetts

"*Integrity Matters* is a powerful call for the return to values such as trust, honesty, graciousness and partnership....This is a must read for those who would lead America into the new millennium."
> — JAC FITZ-ENZ, PH.D., Chief Executive Officer, Human Capital Source,
> and Founder, Saratoga Institute, San Jose, California

"*Integrity Matters* appears to be both inspiring and, of course, very informative. Congratulations on the achievement of this excellent text...."
> — ROBERT W. GALVIN, Chairman Emeritus, Motorola, Inc., Schaumburg, Illinois

"Wouldn't it be great if...society employed the eight attributes outlined by Jim and Dan?"
> — ANTON H. "TONY" GEORGE, President and Chief Executive Officer,
> Indianapolis Motor Speedway LLC, and Indy Racing League LLC,
> Indianapolis, Indiana

"This is just what is needed to address the dramatic decline of values in the United States. It is a road map for managers at all levels to build a solid ethical foundation for their business, enabling companies to regain the trust of their stakeholders...."
> — DAVID A. HANDORF, San Jose, California

"Mirror, mirror on the wall, watch our integrity and don't let it fall. ...*Integrity Matters* gives fascinating insight into the world of integrity; integrity not as a theory, but as a way of life."
> — EHUD HAR-CHEN, executive, electronics company, Tel Aviv, Israel

"*Integrity Matters* is just what America needs right now—a refresher course in basic values.... Find out why it pays to put integrity back into your life. Read *Integrity Matters* to get back where we belong."
> — ROGER HARNED, PH.D., interior design and international publications,
> Carmel, California

"This book will help you relate to your own value system and to how values drive integrity."
> — GLEN H. HINER, Pebble Beach, California

"This is a topic that needs to be incorporated into every institution in the U.S. The lack of integrity seems to have infected every type of institution, and almost all of them first respond in a self-defense mode."
> — DONALD E. HOLT, Jensen Beach, Florida

"This book should be on every CEO's office table, with well-worn pages."
> — COL. (RETIRED) DAVID W. HUNT, D.A.R. Inc., Global Security Consultants,
> Scarborough, Maine

"Integrity-centered leadership is not optional, but mandatory, for leaders of the 21st century."
> — WILLIAM L. HURLEY, Managing Director, Sheraton Resorts Phoenix Seagaia,
> Miyazaki, Japan

"*Integrity Matters* provides clear and insightful guidance on the most crucial issues now facing those institutions upon which our nation depends."
> — ANTHONY T. KARACHALE, Attorney, Monterey, California

"*Integrity Matters* hits upon a way to bring real-life business dilemmas into a crystal clear focus in a manner that raises the quality of thinking about ethical choices in business. ..."
— ROBERT M. KAVNER, former Executive Vice-President and
Chief Financial Officer, AT&T, Carmel, California

"We are in need of reminders of ethical behavior in all forms of organizations and individuals, be they business, religious, charitable, political or volunteering ...."
— RICHARD J. KINZIG, Vice-President of Finance (retired), Palatine, Illinois

"*Integrity Matters* hits the proverbial nail on the head. ...All individuals who continue life-long learning, ought to turn to *Integrity Matters* as a beacon of light in the darkness of ethical uncertainty."
— DONALD C. KLECKNER, PH.D., Redlands, California, former President,
Elmhurst College, and former President, Chapman University

"Jim Bracher and Dan Halloran pull no punches. They are here to tell us what it's really like to lead with integrity on the front lines and in the executive suites of today's complex organizations."
— JAMES M. KOUZES, co-author, *The Leadership Challenge* and *Encouraging the Heart*, and Chairman Emeritus, Tom Peters Company,
San Jose, California

"At a time when America's basic values are eroding and fading into the darkness, Bracher and Halloran...have delivered a blueprint and a challenge to American leaders in all walks of life to step up and make a difference."
— CASEY F. KOZIOL, Vice-President of Human Resources (retired), Motorola, Inc.,
Scottsdale, Arizona

"In *Integrity Matters*, Bracher and Halloran make the point that, in the end, integrity pays. Ultimately, lack of integrity is revealed and the damage, often to the innocent, is destructive. Integrity is the cement holding together the building blocks of our society and its economy ...."
— PETER LARR, Rye, New York

"The old saying 'You can't be a little pregnant' applies to how you act, write, speak, 24/7. Eighty percent adherence to integrity just won't cut it. *Integrity Matters* goes to the core of our need for trust from our leaders and our institutions. The message needs to be absorbed into what we expect from ourselves and from others ...."
— HERBERT E. LISTER, Pebble Beach, California

"Read *Integrity Matters* now! ...There is real hope for those who seek honesty, ethics and just plain decency in the world. ...This book should serve as a wake-up call to those who would preserve our personal and commercial freedoms."
— MARK W. LORIMER, President, Lorimer Associates, former President and
Chief Executive Officer, Autobytel Inc., former Partner,
Dewey Ballantine LLC, San Clemente, California

"*Integrity Matters* is a clarion call to arms in the face of a society which is loath to focus on individual responsibility ... it offers an antidote to many of the ills which currently face us, individually, nationally and internationally."
— CHARLES E. H. LUEDDE, Attorney, St. Louis, Missouri

"What *Integrity Matters* reminds me to do is look into that mirror of life, and ask myself, 'Am I doing the honest things in business that I should, when nobody else is looking?' Even though it's been said many times over, it's always good to be sure you're treating people the way you hope to be treated. At the end of the day, *Integrity Matters* reminds me to act upon that rule."
> — WILLIAM RAMSEY, Owner/Partner, Mann Packing Company Inc.,
> Salinas, California

"This material should be taught in every college business curriculum."
> — KARL J. REICHARDT, R & K Associates, Tempe, Arizona

"The thoughtful discourse in *Integrity Matters*...on the many facets of institutional and personal integrity, makes one acutely aware of the importance of integrity at every level to the long-term viability and profitability of a corporation."
> — TONI REMBE, Attorney, San Francisco, California

"*Integrity Matters* is an incredibly ambitious and bold book. Jim Bracher and Dan Halloran have offered a proposal for dealing with the moral decline in this country—which has afflicted all of us—including institutions such as government, church and business. ...It is must reading for all who are concerned about the moral dry rot that is the subject of media exposure....Jim and Dan have done a great service in showing us the path to the restoration of integrity. The responsibility is now ours to follow it."
> — THE HONORABLE CHARLES B. RENFREW, former United States Federal Judge;
> former Deputy Attorney General of the United States; former Vice-President,
> Legal Affairs, Chevron Corporation, San Francisco, California

"Wow! Wow! Wow! What a book! *Integrity Matters* is so powerful that it defies description! ...It will not only change every person and organization, but also our country. There will be a return to greatness through integrity...."
> — FRED A. RIDDLE, DDS, Iowa City, Iowa

"*Integrity Matters* contains valuable messages for all segments of society—teenagers, senior managers and the general public."
> — C. KENNETH ROBERTS, General Counsel (retired), Houston, Texas

"Integrity matters when you start and end your day and everything in between....I recommend it for anyone who wants to make a positive difference in their future."
> — JOHN E. RODENHAUSEN, Chief Operating Officer, Tricon North America Inc.,
> Carlsbad, California

"*Integrity Matters*, built upon the eight attributes of integrity, clearly describes the values to which all should aspire...."
> — PEG AND JOHN ROYSE, Sanibel Island, Florida

"*Integrity Matters* tackles the big enchilada in a culture in transition, namely the erosion of integrity in our institutions, our organizations and our businesses, as well as those individuals whose task it is to lead them....Ethical clarity emerges as the authors give new meaning to common sense, all of it delivered with a sense of urgency...."
> — AMBASSADOR ROBERT A. SEIPLE, Founder and Chairman of the Board,
> Institute for Global Engagement, Centreville, Maryland

"*Integrity Matters* is ... a rich resource that captures complex ideas in a concise, interactive dialogue format; useful for anyone or any organization to reset their ethical compass and reroute their ethical behaviors toward integrity-centered practices."
> — LAVKUMAR SHELAT, Toronto, Canada

"Integrity DOES matter. It always has, of course, but in today's environment of mistrust of many of our institutions and leaders, it takes on new relevance in our daily lives....I recommend *Integrity Matters* to anyone concerned about integrity today, which should be everybody."
> — VAN SKILLING, Skilling Enterprises, former Chief Executive Officer of
> Experian Information Solutions Inc. (formerly TRW Credit Services),
> Palm Desert, California

"*Integrity Matters* by Jim Bracher and Dan Halloran reminds readers that honoring commitments and treating people properly are the right things to do and the most productive and profitable way to operate...."
> — ANDREW C. "ANDY" SMITH, Andrew Smith Company, Salinas, California

"*Integrity Matters* is interesting and challenging...guaranteed to make you think, hard, about integrity in America today."
> — PETER P. SMITH, Ph.D., President, California State University, Monterey Bay,
> Seaside, California

"Practical, timely and much-needed guidance abounds in this well-written book. A 'must read' for all Chief Financial Officers."
> — SAM SRINIVASAN, Founder, Health Language.com,
> and former Chief Financial Officer, Cirrus Logic, Fremont, California

"One of the great gifts of *Integrity Matters* is that it deals with the realm of the possible. Not ethereal. Not out of reach. But right in front of you, possible, step by step, until individuals, governments, organizations remember how to walk straight up and ahead."
> — THE RT. REV. WILLIAM E. SWING, Bishop, Episcopal Diocese of California,
> San Francisco, California

"Integrity—or 'Holding Fast to the Source' as the ancient sages of the East put it—has been of utmost relevance since the dawn of civilization. Sometimes, though, we lose sight of it. Jim Bracher and Dan Halloran remind us that INTEGRITY MATTERS...!
> — GEORGE E. SYCIP, San Francisco, California

"One of the biggest challenges in changing the world is that a small percentage of people do break the rules and 'get away with it.' This seduces a few more. This is not a reason to quit trying. ...If you want to run a prosperous business for the long-run and like what you see when you look in the mirror, live your life by the principles in this book!"
> — FRANK L. TODD, retired senior executive, Barrington, Illinois

"Jim Bracher and Dan Halloran have in this book, *Integrity Matters*, given new and relevant reinforcement to the idea that honesty is the best policy."
> — SANDER VANOCUR, Santa Barbara, California

"*Integrity Matters* is clearly NOT just another business behavior doctrine. It provides principles that can be used in all aspects of our lives. And it demonstrates the magnitude of how much influence one individual can have in a society. ...The road from trustworthiness to deception is paved with 'one compromise at a time.' Within all of the recent business scandals, we can see the collective impact of such compromises. ...Following the framework provided by Jim and Dan in this book, we, as individuals, can help restore the trust that we as a society allowed to deteriorate in the first place."
　　— MARY D. WALTUCK, Beesley Associates, Inc., Boston, Massachusetts

"*Integrity Matters* provides a basis for discussion that can be useful as a reference in instruction. Ethical dilemmas are often not easily or clearly solved by rules or guidelines, thus the premises presented offer great discussion points...."
　　— COLLETTE E. WIGGINS, Director of Human Resources, Barrington, Illinois

"The health of our free market system and of society in general may well depend on the extent to which we learn the lessons this little book teaches us."
　　— JAMES W. WILSON, Austin, Texas

"Jim and Dan take aim at the fallacy that 'greed is good.' In a back-to-basics tour de force, they challenge us to re-orient our localized thinking, providing frameworks that emphasize the need for integrity in business and life. They underline that this not only matters, but our futures depend on it."
　　— PHILIP J. WILSON, PH.D., Chief Executive Officer, Adeptra Ltd.,
　　　Reading, Berkshire, England

"Foundational reading for Marriage and Family Counselors and for those in the helping professions, this book is about enhancing relationships via integrity. ...A valuable resource for us...as we support our clients who seek guidance, as business owners, employees, partners and parents, in our changing world."
　　— JUDITH YEAGER, Marriage and Family Counselor, Founder,
　　　Gestalt Therapy Training Institute, Las Vegas, Nevada

Full-length endorsements are online at:
www.integritymatters.com and www.torchlight.com

INTEGRITY MATTERS

INTEGRITY MATTERS

James F. Bracher • Daniel E. Halloran

TORCHLIGHT PUBLISHING, INC.

shifting the paradigm

First Printing 2004

Design by Bookwrights
Printed in the United States of America

Published simultaneously in the United States of America and Canada by Torchlight Publishing, Inc.

Library of Congress Cataloging-in-Publication Data

Bracher, James F., 1945-
  Integrity Matters / by James F. Bracher and Daniel E. Halloran.
    p. cm.
Advice based on similar examples from their weekly newspaper column,"Integrity Matters," in *The Californian*, a daily newspaper based in Salinas, California.
  ISBN 1-887089-03-9
1. Leadership. 2. Integrity. 3. Business ethics. 4. Social ethics.
5. Organizational behavior. I. Halloran, Daniel E., 1939- II. Title.
HD57.7.B695 2004
658.4'092–dc22
                              2003025288

Attention Colleges, Universities, Corporations, Associations and Professional Organizations: *Integrity Matters* is available at special discounts for bulk purchases for training, sales promotions, premiums, fund-raising or educational use. Special books, booklets or excerpts can be created to suit your specific needs.

For information, contact the Publisher:

TORCHLIGHT PUBLISHING, INC.
shifting the paradigm

P.O. Box 52, Badger CA 93603
Phone: (559) 337-2200 • Fax: (559) 337-2354
E-mail: torchlight@spiralcomm.net • www.torchlight.com

Dedication

For our children and grandchildren,
and the grandchildren of our grandchildren.

Acknowledgements

Writing *Integrity Matters* provided us with an opportunity to incorporate inherited values from our respective families, which we have refined through our own experience. We appreciate the ideas, assistance, patience and perspective of trusted family members, friends and associates. Combining their input with the expertise and able support of professionals in the publishing field has enabled us to make our cultural concern, namely, the expansion of an "integrity" conversation, into the reality of this book.

Foremost among those we thank are Jane Bracher and Toni Halloran, who remain role models of integrity for each of us. Every step of the way they helped us work through the issues and challenges related to the writing of *Integrity Matters*. They were and are the motivation behind the mission to improve the world in which we live. Also, we offer our thanks to Ruby Sanchez, our office assistant. She helped us to manage multiple time-consuming priorities as we addressed the demands of writing, while not ignoring the requirements of serving clients graciously.

As the manuscript progressed, a number of friends and associates were kind enough to offer their constructive and insightful recommendations, and in some cases provided written endorsements. We thank every contributor: Alvin Achenbaum, Nancy Albertini, Jim Austgen, Bill Barnett, Paul Baszucki, Garm Beall, Pete Bogda, Peter Burwash, Jim Carr, Ken Cavallaro, Bob Coon, Gary Coughlan, Jozen Cummings, Steve Dart, Claire and Jack Davis, Martha Dennis, Rich Divelbiss, Lacy Edwards, Bob Fain, Scott Faust, Vaughn Feather, George Fisher, Jac Fitz-enz, Bob Galvin, Tony George, Kim Greer, Dave Handorf, Peter Hannaford, Ehud Har-Chen, Roger Harned, Glen Hiner, Don Holt, David Hunt, Bill Hurley, Tony Karachale, Bob Kavner, Dick Kinzig, Donald Kleckner, Jim Kouzes, Casey Koziol, Peter Larr, Herb Lister, Charles Loew, Mark Lorimer, Charles Luedde, David Lyon, John Mallard, Steve Metzger, Bert Millen, Basil Mills, Larry Minnich, Rich Moran, Phil Nienstedt, Jock Ochiltree, Tom Paulick, Bob Placko, Cody Plott, Bill Ramsey, Karl Reichardt, Toni Rembe, Charles Renfrew, Fred Riddle, Kenneth Roberts, John Rodenhausen, Peg and John Royse, Bob Seiple, Lavkumar Shelat, Van Skilling, Andy Smith, Peter Smith, Sam Srinivasan, Bishop William Swing, George SyCip, Frank Todd, Sander Vanocur, Mary Waltuck, Scott Warrington, Collette Wiggins, Jim Wilson, Phil Wilson and Judith Yeager.

We are especially appreciative of the encouragement, guidance and opportunities provided by Scott Faust, executive editor, and Tim Dowd, president and publisher, of *The Californian* and *El Sol* newspapers in Salinas, California. In addition, we thank the following for their professional assistance: Lewis Leader, who consulted with us early in our efforts, and later, Laurie Gibson, who ably assisted with content, format and language; Mayapriya Long and Elizabeth Coffey for their design of the cover and interior of the book; and Gary Aleksiewicz, who provided the indexing. Of course, we are appreciative of our publisher, Alister Taylor, for his support, experience and planning along the way.

Because of this excellent group of individuals, we are made wiser and more capable of leaving a legacy for constructive cultural change. We are committed to continue expanding the "integrity conversation" in every way that we can. We hope and believe that *Integrity Matters* will have a lasting impact.

With appreciation,
JIM BRACHER AND DAN HALLORAN

Contents

Foreword
by Peter D. Hannaford

In an age steeped in moral relativism and easy-going ethics, it is not surprising to find that the Chief Executive Officer of a large corporation stands trial for looting the treasury of his publicly traded company. And recently, that a number of mutual fund managers and currency traders have been indicted for fleecing investors of a large amount of money over a period of years. Nor is it all that surprising to find that a President has sex with an intern in the Oval Office and lies about it.

What has happened to integrity in American life? It has been taking a beating—and a big one—for three decades or so. The erosion of standards of behavior (a result of the assault on respect for authority that began in the 1960's) has, in turn, eroded the concept of conscience and has all but eliminated shame as a factor in one's behavior. How can one be ashamed of breaking standards of behavior if there are none to break?

While it may seem that the "anything goes" approach to life is unstoppable, there are many people who still believe that standards of behavior, conscience and integrity are essential if we are to have a moral and just society. Certainly, the readers of Jim Bracher's newspaper column, "Integrity Matters," believe that. And, for every individual who writes in to ask him a question about integrity, there must be thousands who share those same concerns.

You will meet a number of such readers in this book, written by Jim and his colleague Dan Halloran. The answers Jim gives to his readers' questions amount to common sense guidelines through the minefield of moral relativism and "situation ethics."

This book will show you the steps to take to ensure that your business, civic organization or volunteer group can operate with high standards of integrity. The companion question to "Whatever happened to integrity?" is "How can we get it back?" The authors have the answer, and it is yours for the reading—and to implement.

Peter D. Hannaford is the author of nine books (seven about U.S. Presidents) and numerous articles. He has worked in the profession of public affairs for more than 30 years.

Preface

"In evaluating people you look for three qualities:
integrity, intelligence, and energy.
And if you don't have the first, the other two will kill you."
–Warren Buffett, Omaha World-Herald

There is a great need to restore integrity in our society. We've learned that when businesses fail in their values, they decay from the inside. In the late 1990s, values came to be viewed as expensive, conservative relics of the old economy. In the race to drive up stock prices by any means available, false promises of hollow values spoke too frequently to what would not—or could not—be done. As the 21st century begins, the excesses of a few appear to have punished nearly all elements of society, especially the economy. A world has been created where the prevailing structures promote the politics of convenience over the commitment of leadership. Too many have enjoyed the excesses of luxury while drifting from quick deals to outright dishonesty.

Today, public scandals continue to erode faith and confidence in political leaders, religious institutions, law enforcement, the educational system and the free market itself. The good news is that this avalanche of bad news has generated a willingness to discuss ethics and values, both within organizations and on a personal level. We are determined to keep this new conversation going. This book examines ethical challenges arising in public and private arenas, and presents practical, integrity-centered responses from the "Integrity Matters" newspaper column.

Jim Bracher has invested his most recent 23 years as a consultant on integrity-centered leadership. Beginning in 2002, he created a weekly newspaper column, "Integrity Matters," in *The Californian*, a daily newspaper based in Salinas, California. These columns, which respond to concerns raised by newspaper readers and visitors to the Bracher Center website, www.brachercenter.com, form the foundation of our efforts toward restoring integrity in our society.

Jim's venture into column writing was precipitated in part by his founding, in 2002, of the Bracher Center for Integrity in Leadership, based in Monterey, California. The Center is an extension of his 33 years of advising individuals and organizations. Jim founded his executive leadership company, Dimension Five Consultants, Inc., (of which he is also chairman) in 1980. Prior to the establishment of Dimension Five, he served as a chaplain, associate minister and senior pastor for 10 years. He remains committed to helping individual leaders and organizations' leadership teams operate effectively while expanding the dialogue on business integrity.

Our professional relationship began in January 1983, when my employer asked me to assume the responsibilities of human resources for a new subsidiary that was already one of Jim's corporate clients. The speed, accuracy and effectiveness of his communication were most beneficial. My respect for him increased as we worked together, and our relationship grew on both the professional and personal levels. I found his efforts to restore integrity in business to be relevant and meaningful.

We remained in contact following my retirement in 2001. A few months later, Jim asked me to join him in establishing the Bracher Center for Integrity in Leadership. At first I was reluctant, wanting instead to retire to a life of golf, travel and entertainment. But the many corporate scandals of this period, coupled with the good counsel of my wife, Toni, convinced me that helping Jim was the right thing to do.

Jim's core principle is that integrity is essential for rebuilding the foundation of our economy, even our society. Clearly, the time for restoring trust is now. Our goal at the Center is to restore integrity through insight. By providing integrity-centered counsel, we are working to build a world in which people do what they say they will do and are forthright in their communications; where a handshake solidifies any promise.

The questions posed to the "Integrity Matters" newspaper column, and the Bracher responses, address some recent painful revelations that indicate the need for the restoration of trust. It is time to strengthen the way that businesses and other institutions operate and how they communicate with their customers, investors, employees, communities and the general public. The issues raised can furnish answers that, if not quite universal, have broad relevance to values and decisions—for individuals, for organizations and for society.

Our free markets, combined with our personal freedoms and the rule of law, have set the United States apart from other countries. Business is the engine that built this nation; it continues to sustain our society. Business transactions are building blocks for trust. The mission of this book, as well as the Center, is to restore trust in the foundations of society through counsel that will re-ignite integrity-centered leadership. *Integrity Matters* provides guidance constructed around eight integrity-centered attributes, discussed in Chapters 4 through 11.

The Eight Attributes provide definition, structure and direction for individuals, organizations and society in the formation of trust in relationships. Business partnerships in the broadest sense, just as personal relationships, require consistent performance demonstrating the elements we address in the following pages.

The columns utilized in this book were written in response to questions posed by either a reader of *The Californian* or a visitor to the Bracher Center website. The Bracher replies to the candid questions conduct readers on a guided tour of current issues of concern in the public mind. Also, the responses touch on timeless issues—trust between friends, for example—as well as events in the news, such as baseball slugger Sammy Sosa's corked bat and the death of respected broadcaster David Brinkley. Where appropriate, we have provided context before and after the "Integrity Matters" columns.

It is no accident that the columns and this book follow a question-and-reply format. Open and ongoing conversations engage readers with writers. This type of dialogue will help to replenish and revive fundamental values relating to integrity—in business, in organizations and in personal relationships. This book brings the columns together in a series of straightforward lessons about how to do the right thing.

We expect this book to help people in their efforts to restore confidence in the leadership of our society's institutions. We want to encourage our readers to take appropriate "self-regulating" actions to restore trust, both interpersonally and economically.

Surely, we are tired of the scandals that have shaken faith in elected officials, law enforcement, religious institutions and corporate leadership. A movement to restore values in the cherished structures of our society is overdue, and it will likely be welcomed by many, if not most, of our communities. Trust can—and must—be restored. The time to restore our "integrity-centered house" is now.

DANIEL E. HALLORAN
Monterey, California
October 30, 2003

Chapter 1
Integrity: Where Did It Go?

Integrity is one of several paths; it distinguishes itself
from the others because it is the right path and the only one
upon which you will never get lost.
– M.H. McKee

We have written this book because the greatness of the United States as a nation, the prosperity and opportunities we have enjoyed, will be lost to the children of our own children unless we put an end to the progressive decay in our values that is rotting our society from within. Our loss of trust in our nation's institutions—our political leaders, spiritual mentors, Wall Street and even our neighbors on "Main Street"—has reached a critical and dangerous level. Even our global friends have learned to mistrust our intentions. The future of our free market system, as we have known it, may be in more jeopardy from the loss of integrity within, than from any terrorist threat we face.

By highlighting integrity we intend to leave a legacy in which honesty is once again rewarded. We recognize that public employment needs to be pursued as a service and not as a safe haven for the underqualified. We want to help parents teach accountability to their children—and to model it for them in practice. We want to help create a tradition in which businesspeople with a solid ethical foundation are the norm. It used to be that way. It can be so again! It is our obligation, having raised the issue, to provide a roadmap for this journey. Integrity-centered leadership, our focus, can be defined as follows:

1. Parents and families for the next generation, to provide unconditional love and acceptance, while nurturing socially responsive values;

2. Educators for students, to enable learning for all who seek to grow their minds;

3. Spiritual counselors for believers, to exhibit and live their messages;

4. Elected and appointed employees of the government for their constituents, to transcend self-serving goals and truly serve all of the people;

5. Celebrities and public figures for their fans, to model admirable behaviors, including appreciation, humility and self-discipline;

6. Bosses for their teams, to build a healthy environment for productivity.

And there is reason for hope.

Generally speaking, people *are* trustworthy. Doctors prescribe the correct medicines; pharmacists fill their prescriptions accurately. We trust this, and we act on that trust. Every day, we trust that certain things will happen, some of them so small we don't give them a second thought in the United States. Newspapers are delivered on our doorsteps or driveways as promised. Drivers stop when traffic lights turn red. Waiters and waitresses serve good food, and return the correct change to us after a meal. We are surrounded by integrity issues every day. Our continued successful resolution of these issues provides a basis for the renewal of our society. *Integrity Matters* offers a platform upon which this conversation can be expanded. In this country, we are fortunate to have conditions of trust and integrity still in place. For us, life tends to work itself out.

Yet all is not well. The clouds on our horizon are much like the ominous off-shore image of an approaching category 5 hurricane. And although we are surrounded by integrity issues, at times we are not surrounded by—or imbued with—integrity itself. Integrity is eroding in American society, and if we do not find a way to rebuild it, we will continue down a slippery slope that will lead to the sacrifice of the freedoms that we know and enjoy. If we choose the lowest common denominator with regard to values, then we jeopardize the well-being of our children and our children's children by eroding the trust that glues our society together—one compromise at a time.

Up to now, our representative form of democracy has preserved the state of our republic through a four-way balance of power. Congress is able to respond to the public's needs with legislation; the President and Executive Branch have the power to administer the law; the Supreme Court is the final arbiter in judging the constitutionality of our government's actions; and the "fourth estate," our free press, has the ability to keep the actions of the other three groups (as well as itself) in the spotlight. For more than 225 years, this balance of power has prevented the actualization of British Professor Alexander Tyler's 1778 judgments regarding democracy, which are detailed in his comments on the fall of Athenian democracy in ancient Greece:

> A democracy cannot exist as a permanent form of government. It can only exist until the voters discover that they can vote themselves money from the public treasure. From that moment on the majority always votes for the candidates promising the most money from the public treasury, with the result that a democracy always collapses over loose fiscal policy followed by a dictatorship.
>
> The average age of the world's great civilizations has been two hundred years. These nations have progressed through the following sequence:
>
> from bondage to spiritual faith,
> from spiritual faith to great courage,
> from courage to liberty,
> from liberty to abundance,
> from abundance to selfishness,
> from selfishness to complacency,
> from complacency to apathy,
> from apathy to dependency,
> from dependency back to bondage.[1]

But make no mistake. Professor Tyler's insights have alarming parallels to the progression of our own society! We have thus far avoided the final deterioration because our society has been one in which Congress has acted to correct abuses, even the abuses of its own. Individuals have been free to act as they choose so long as they did not—and do not—infringe upon the rights of others. These rights are defined in the Constitution, the Bill of Rights and subsequent legislation based in common law. But we are on a treadmill of corrective legislation that has at its very roots the avoidance of accountability and the securing of the lowest-common-denominator principle in the construction of our future. Further, every time public outcry compels Congress to pass a new law, it results in additional constraints upon freedom. Sometimes this is necessary, as can be seen by the legislation in response to the events of September 11, 2001. The risk lies, however, in the cumulative legislation that would arise from the gradual collapse of our values—a process we believe has begun to accelerate. When legislation is implemented to counteract failed self-regulation, the result can be cumbersome, creating excessive bureaucracy with its own unanticipated consequences.

The increase of government payroll and expenditures of tax-supported (and deficit-generating) agencies is significant, as given witness by the newly created Cabinet-level organization of Homeland Security, which arose because of the failure of law enforcement agencies to cooperate with each other (regulate themselves) in the nation's interest. Other examples include the National Transportation Safety Board and the more established Food and Drug Administration. While no one would argue with the need for these agencies, they each have their origin in a failure of self-regulation of an industry or government group—in security, in transportation and in the food and pharmaceuticals that we consume. These agencies are regulatory, and therefore restrict freedom. These agencies do not generate production; they do not in themselves add to the economic power of this nation. We may very much appreciate their contributions, but each agency consumes tax dollars.

When the revenue collected by the government falls short of the consumptive needs of federal, state and local government payments, we call it a deficit. When the deficit caused by these regulatory payments becomes so large that the tax potential even under the best assumptions is unable to cope with its inflation, we will have a mess. Such an economic trauma does not need to occur, but it could if the tendency to rely upon regulatory legislation increases, as it has been. With each new law we have an example of the erosion of trust in others, and further restriction of freedom. Without positive, preventative actions, there is the real potential to move from liberty to bondage, in our generation, as described by Tyler more than two centuries ago.

Of course, public scandals have been followed by legislative responses many times in our nation's history. The obvious fact of scandal is not new. Human nature is imperfect. We cannot remember a time, however, when virtually every one of our nation's basic structural institutions has been so engulfed in violating the honorable expectations of the public. Scandals are becoming so common that the word itself has lost its emotional heat. Recent betrayals of trust at the organizational level include the following examples:

The public's trust in the media was damaged in 2003 by the fall of *The New York Times'* executive editor and his favored journalist because of the uproar caused by the latter's plagiarism and fabrication scandal. Part of the nation's spiritual confidence has been shaken by the irresponsible behavior of a number of religious leaders. The Roman Catholic Church has begun working its way—secretively at first and awkwardly at best—through a staggering number of pedophile cases that appear to have been dragged out by the legal system and a church hierarchy operating in either hypocrisy or denial. That the Roman

Catholic Church will eventually right itself is not questioned—but the cost in trust has been high. We've also learned that powerful political figures (at and near the top of national leadership) can lie under oath, and quibble over the meaning of words, rather than own up to confidence-destroying behavior. We could refer to this period in our history as "the death of American innocence."

Frustration over this loss of trust was replaced by fear when millions of people watched the meltdown of the pension funds and retirement dreams of thousands of employees in several highly visible public companies. We listened with amazement as the Enron story unfolded; the Chief Executive Officer professing ignorance about the schemes his Chief Financial Officer was utilizing, or even about how the company he led was operating. We sympathized with the employees of Arthur Andersen who lost their jobs as that accounting firm was driven out of business because of the behavior of a relative few. The Sarbanes-Oxley Act of 2002 was quickly constructed and passed as a response to those corporate scandals; it is one of the more recent examples of legislation written because business leaders failed to act responsibly.

The Sarbanes-Oxley Act of 2002 represents the primary legislative response to recent corporate scandals such as Enron, as well as that of the WorldCom and Adelphia financial frauds, among other examples of corporate, institutional and individual misconduct. The Act creates the new Public Company Accounting Oversight Board to establish and monitor auditing and accounting standards emphasizing auditor independence, consistency and integrity, and is discussed in more depth in the next chapter. Every time Congress passes a law to overcome any lack of self-regulation, free markets must cope with an increasing mountain of restrictions on freedoms, in addition to more bureaucratic requirements due to the intended—and unintended—consequences of those laws.

Sadly, the story of senior management's failure of judgment was repeated in several more major cases, including that of a long-established major airline. When the company was under bankruptcy protection, its employees rebelled upon learning that, while they were being asked to take huge pay cuts, the executive row was feathering its nest with pension and bonus guarantees. We have also watched from our living rooms as the household name of homemaking stepped down as Chief Executive Officer of her own high-profile public company due to an insider trading probe.

Obviously, integrity is not just a theoretical concept that has no practical ramifications. Throughout history, lapses of integrity have proven fatal. A recent example is the case of Endovascular Technologies, which pleaded guilty in federal court in July 2003 to 10 felony counts and agreed to pay $92.4 million to settle criminal and civil charges that it covered up thousands of incidents, including 12 deaths, involving one of its surgical products. This lawsuit was actually a grouping of cases in which a medical device called a stent (used to treat heart aneurysms) malfunctioned.[2]

Clearly, our national patience has been tested. Just as clearly, the concern for the integrity of our institutions continues to escalate. In the preceding paragraphs, we have intended to paint a compelling portrait of our society's current situation. We turn our attention next to the processes that operate to correct the abuses that arise from a failure of self-regulation, highlighting some examples of significant upheavals and the corresponding societal responses. In later chapters we address ways to overcome these processes and preserve our nation's freedoms for succeeding generations.

NOTES

1   *The Cycle of Democracy,* by Alexander Fraser Tyler, England, 1778.

2   "Guidant subsidiary pleads guilty in cover-up" Associated Press, June 13, 2003, San Francisco.

Chapter 2

Legislated Integrity:
A Recipe for Failure

That government is best which governs least,
because its people discipline themselves.
– Thomas Jefferson

There are many systems of government in the countries of the world: dictator-ship, monarchy, state collective, democracy, etc. Similarly, a variety of economic systems exist, ranging from state run to free market. Some governments, like Zimbabwe, tax by decree, and provide for the rest of society through patronage. Others, such as China, leave much of the economy free, yet are concerned with political control to such an extent that neighbors may not feel comfortable speak-ing freely to each other about political issues. India and the United Kingdom attempt to be responsive to the will of the governed through an elective process. Yet, in all of these countries, we find the poor (in some cases begging from passersby), who sometimes live just a few miles—or blocks—from ornate six-bed-room mansions. The purpose here is not to pronounce judgment on social and economic systems, although the authors acknowledge a strong preference for the democratic process. However, there is a need to encourage self-regulation in order to retain even the imperfect governments and economic systems we have.

One of our readers was concerned with this very broad issue of whether our free market system is the best one available, most likely as a result of recent scandals.

Dear Jim:

Is there possibly an economic system that is not so structurally flawed that it can result in a society that places its priority on leadership with integrity? Unregulated capitalism clearly results in an unfair con-centration of wealth. Government regulation of a capitalistic system has clearly not been working in recent years, if it ever did, for reasons you have given to narrower questions. Socialism, democratic or otherwise, clearly results in concentration of wealth and power in a few government bureaucrats. How could we build an economic system that rewards integrity and ability at the same time so that those qualities are inherent in our leaders?

Response:

Regarding structurally flawed economic systems and the ways integrity can improve them. First, structures are human. Humans are flawed. However, flaws, if properly addressed, can become strengths.

There is a statement that may have come from a philosopher, a rogue or someone hoping to find a "great" deal: "You cannot cheat an honest person!" These words sound naïve. They may or may not be valid. They do, however, prompt us to reflect on recent business scandals. Were the deals "too good to be true"? If they were, whose motives were flawed? The buyers? Perhaps. The sellers? Probably.

Those in authority who intentionally promise too much are hiding behind their own fears that the truth will not be adequate. The actions of too many who are in high-powered roles seem to be saying, "If 15 per-cent return is not attractive enough for investors, then why not adjust financial reporting procedures to convince the public (buyers and investors) that more should be possible?" "Rat race" (over promising) behaviors are offering false hopes. Too many well-intentioned individu-als feel they are careening wildly over the high cliffs of lying and cheat-ing. The vehicle of commerce has been moving at uncontrolled speeds and the passengers are scared.

Perhaps it is a truth that you cannot cheat an honest human being. Trust is broken between and among the various participants and partners of the free market (stakeholders) when we allow our officials (academic, economic, political and spiritual) to feed us "lines" of comfortable (and dishonest) clichés. Traditional economic controls (the brakes) are broken. Passengers, those buying and investing, have lost confidence. They are casting about for sound and dependable counsel, financial and beyond. Passengers are flailing ... out of fear, mistrust, uncertainty and doubt. Such flailing energizes downturns that lead toward recessions and depressions.

The answer has been and will remain that "It should be common knowledge that free markets must regulate themselves or governments will." Bottom line: wisdom from the philosopher M.H. McKee: "Integrity is one of several paths; it distinguishes itself from the others because it is the right path and the only one upon which you will never get lost."

Through legislative response to popular concerns, America continues to try to perfect itself. The question for all of us is whether the cumulative trend of our legislative changes is moving our society in the right direction.

Placing America and this question in the mirror of the world, we have learned that we are viewed as the land of a second chance, where people have the freedom to succeed or fail. Most people take advantage of this freedom by succeeding to one degree or another, while others fail. A male engineer returning to his Asia-Pacific homeland from an expatriate assignment in the United States reported that the singular freedom that impressed him most about this country was that he could step out on Sunrise Boulevard in Plantation, Florida, and yell that our President is a crook, and know that nothing bad would happen to him; traffic notwithstanding. In his homeland, he would not dare to raise his voice against the government, even with his neighbor. Another Asian expatriate living in the United States commented that in her native country, if you fail to complete your university education, there is no hope for a professional career. She made this observation while enrolled in the university system of the United States, and expressed appreciation for the educational opportunity provided in this nation. In her home country she would have been unable to attend a university at this middle stage in her life, as such opportunities exist only for "fast track" students, and then only as they emerge from secondary schools.

Viewed by these expatriates and by most historians over the 200-plus years of our history, it can be argued that our system of freedoms is doing reasonably well.

As a society, we have been concerned with the question of whether we should expand our social structure to take from those who are able, and provide for those who are not, while preserving the ability for those with initiative to rise as far economically as their talents and opportunities could take them. Balancing free markets against social responsibility is a difficult issue. It is legitimate to worry about the long-term effect of creating confidence-eroding dependencies. Over time, however, the bureaucracy supporting social and regulatory legislation has resulted in a government that is far more intrusive than the one described by Thomas Jefferson in the opening quotation of this chapter.

Government jobs do not typically produce tangible goods. These jobs must be paid for by a tax on the income, capital, goods or services of those who do produce. Yet the erosion of trust present in our society resulting from the excesses of those who refuse to regulate their own behavior represents a real risk to our survival. If we can accomplish our societal goals without creating more government regulatory and welfare bureaucracy than we can afford (either financially or structurally), our system will likely survive. It is the contention of this book that a sound set of integrity-centered values is critical to achieving such a balance.

Our Constitution and structure of laws, checks and balances is very much like the structure of a house that provides operating freedom for the occupants within—in fact, President Lincoln used such an analogy for our nation in rebuking slavery in 1858 when he uttered the famous phrase "A house divided against itself cannot stand."[1] Today we may think of the decaying values that have brought so many scandals to the fore in recent years. We may ponder the risk that our house of government may fall down from the neglect of our own values, the lack of self-regulation as it results in a progression of legislative initiatives, and the weight of the bureaucracy that results.

Our form of government is of, by and for the people, and as such is responsive to the prevailing opinions of the public. To the extent that public opinion is capturing a legitimate need, this is a wonderful system. Even better, our form of government allows the people to compel the correction of a legislative error, or to change a law that has become obsolete, or even an obstacle to progress—if they only will. This process has been masterful, and in itself is not of concern so long as it is used responsibly. At the same time, there are occasions when the public mood is responding to an emotional appeal over an issue that may not be permanent, and causes Congress to respond with legislation that can have unanticipated effects. In virtually all cases of major legislation, and often the result of even minor legislation, the acts of Congress generate tax-funded jobs, agencies and departments that add to the burden of bureaucracy, which is borne by our free market system and the public.

Sometimes this Congressional response to public demand is constructive, a worthwhile investment of the public's money (e.g., the Federal Reserve System), and sometimes it is destructive (e.g., Prohibition, as addressed on pages 12-13). In a significant number of the areas over which Congress has passed regulating action, a strong case can be made that if our institutional leaders would simply behave with common sense and integrity, we might have avoided costly bureaucracy. Most labor and civil rights legislation would seem to fall into this category.

Carrying this thought further, we believe that, to the extent that our society becomes thoughtful and values-focused, the requests made upon Congress will tend to be fewer and better thought-out. The Eight Attributes supporting the theme of this book provide the raw material for developing such an integrity-centered, values-oriented and self-regulating society, which will enable government to do what it does best:

"... provide for the common defense, promote the general welfare, and secure the blessings of liberty to ourselves and our posterity..."

—Preamble to The Constitution of the United States of America

When self-regulation fails, our body politic has, of course, devised a system of laws. When self-regulation fails among companies in our free market system, we know that governmental agencies and/or Congress will step in and pass further regulations and laws to prevent, or provide a remedy to, the damages of corporate abuse. We've seen this over the history of this country. A perceived abuse takes hold in the mind of the public, and Congress acts to pass a law to remedy the situation. Unfortunately, there can be unintended consequences suggesting even more legislation to correct the abuses of the initial regulation. Time passes and circumstances again change. New laws create further unintended consequences, encouraging yet more burdensome legislation. The danger to our society is that the bureaucracy that evolves from this cycle of legislation, consequence and corrective legislation will eventually itself become the problem, and choke the free market system we know today.

If we are to remain the free market "beacon on the hill," we must find a way to reinvigorate our values system to the level where self-regulation occurs. Human nature likely will not change much, but human behavior can—and does—change when value systems capture mind-share and excite the public. The pendulum can swing back in favor of a values-based culture. Commitment to socially responsive values (e.g., character, honesty, openness, partnership, performance, charity and graciousness) is vital. It is at the core of self-regulation. A few brief lessons from history can be used to demonstrate this issue.

In its initial thrust, the public demand for legislation may not insist upon the creation of new bureaucracy, but may impact the values of the nation for generations and most certainly consumes tax dollars that might have been used for other purposes (and in some cases, much better purposes). The controversies that have surrounded aspects of our Pledge of Allegiance are such an example. Written by Mr. Francis Bellamy, the Pledge was first widely used in 1892. Initially, it included no mention of God, even though Bellamy was a Baptist minister. Around 1924, the wording was changed from "my flag" to "the flag of the United States of America." The Pledge had no official standing at that time. It was not until June 22, 1942, that Congress formalized the Pledge, due to the patriotism generated in the midst of World War II. On Flag Day in 1954, Congress added the words "under God" following the words "one nation" when the public was shaken by the Korean War and the specter of the Soviet Union's repression of all forms of religion. The Flag Code then passed by Congress specifies that any further changes must have the approval of the U.S. President.

This saga continues to evolve, of course, and on June 26, 2003, the U.S. Court of Appeals, 9th Circuit (based in San Francisco), ruled in a majority opinion that the reference to God in the Pledge violated the First Amendment's Establishment Clause, which requires the separation of church and state. This decision is not yet binding (as of the writing of this book), in order to give the government time to appeal the case to the U.S. Supreme Court. That very Court ruled in another case during 2003 that the Chief Justice of the Alabama Supreme Court violated the First Amendment to the U.S. Constitution for refusing to remove from the court-house a monument displaying the Bible's Ten Commandments.

Religion, in its various forms, has been the repository of the values on which many societies—including America's—have been created. That these values change over time, for good or ill, can be illustrated by a few examples, one of which is money. Many people today were not yet born when Congress passed legislation requiring that the phrase "In God We Trust" be put on our nation's currency. (In 1955, then President Eisenhower signed Public Law 84-140, which mandated that "In God We Trust" appear on all U.S. currency and coinage.) Today, just as with the preceding discussion concerning the flag, various groups have challenged any reference to God on our nation's money, in the classroom or anywhere else.

Shifts in values have occurred at other times in our nation's history, with greater bureaucratic effect. For example, the personal use of alcohol was per-ceived as an enormous social problem, with campaigns by prohibitionists to close down bars and liquor stores building from Carrie A. Nation's efforts of the early 1900's,[2] and which gave rise to the Volstead Act. Named after its champion, Con-gressman Andrew Volstead of Minnesota, and passed as the 18th Amendment to the U.S. Constitution in 1919, the Volstead Act became law when the required three-fourths of the states ratified it in 1920. This Act prohibited the manufac-ture, distribution and sale of alcoholic beverages.

The law enforcement system was augmented to fight abuses of this new law. However, the enforcement efforts were witness to the "Roaring 20's," where mem-bers of organized crime gained control of the sale and distribution of alcohol. Organized criminal activity became such an enormous social problem, with pub-lic shootings by gangs and highly publicized police raids, that it gave leverage to another shift in values. This shift generated the repeal of this "noble experiment" in the Depression days of 1932, with the 21st Amendment to the Constitution. This is the only time in our history that one constitutional amendment led direct-ly to the canceling of another constitutional amendment a dozen years later.

The atmosphere of excess that existed in the 1920's may have contributed to the "Crash of '29," which itself ushered in the Great Depression of 1929–1941. During this period, unemployment rose above 20 percent in the United States, and the demand for Federal intervention went far beyond anything previously seen. There was an initial rush of legislation that attempted to regulate the financial and securities industries and restore the confidence of the American public. Such regulation of corporations has its basis in common law.[3]

The Reconstruction Finance Corporation was formed in 1932 to rebuild our banking system; that same year the Glass-Stegall Act (designed to protect our financial infrastructure by prohibiting banks, insurance companies and brokerage houses from engaging in each other's services) was passed. The next year saw passage of the Emergency Bank Act, creating the Federal Deposit Insurance Corporation, to insure the public's deposit accounts. This was followed by the Economic Act, and then the Securities Act of 1933 was passed, which in turn was quickly followed and augmented by the Securities and Exchange Act of 1934. These required the formation of the Securities and Exchange Commission (SEC), and registration with the SEC of all securities exchanges, brokers and dealers, with restrictions on behavior (such as margin limits) to protect the public. The intent, of course, was to restore public confidence, and also to avoid another stock market crash of the sort that occurred in October 1929.

This period also gave us the 1933 National Industrial Recovery Act (declared unconstitutional in 1935) and its immediate successor, the National Labor Relations Act of 1935, which protected workers' rights to self-organize. This Act was created following a period of industrial warfare against unionization—which itself was a response to employer exploitation of employees. Workers did organize, but when they did, they were able to form either "closed shops" or "union shops." The closed shop concept required an individual to be a member of the union prior to his or her employment at a company, while the union shop required union membership following a brief period after employment had begun. This pendulum swing of legislation was implemented, and set the stage for the abuses of the closed shop concept. A common practice involved some union stewards demanding up-front payments to facilitate union membership, even before a person could apply for a job in a closed shop. The Taft-Hartley Act was subsequently passed in 1947 with the intention of rebalancing the labor environment by making clear that employees had an equal right *not* to organize, effectively making the closed shop illegal. In general, the Taft-Hartley Act enabled "right-to-work" legislation in those states that chose to enact these laws while still permitting the union shop in the remaining (majority of) states. Right-to-work laws essentially prohibit the union shop in the right-to-work states.

Demonstrating the theme of legislative action, correction and reaction, Congress has amended labor laws several times through the years. The Landrum-Griffen Labor-Management Reporting and Disclosure Act of 1959 addressed pension plan abuses and formalized the right of the construction industry to use the union "hiring hall" arrangement favored by both the industry and the unions. The Civil Rights Act of 1964 and the Equal Pay Act of 1971 are two more examples of legislative intervention. Also created through this series of labor laws were the National Labor Relations Board and the United States Equal Opportunity Commission. These are two organizations that include panels of judges and field investigators, as well as the union election overseers of the National Labor Relations Board. These agencies are funded via the taxes paid by millions of workers, both labor and management.

The Social Security Act was passed in 1935, with the intention of providing a safety net for members of the labor force. This law, too, has been amended many times over the years to reflect the inclusive levels of social responsibility, adding provisions such as Medicare, while increasing both the tax rate to cover the added costs, and broadening the definitions of eligibility to bring more workers under its umbrella.

This form of reactive legislation was demonstrated again in the recent and rapid passage of the Public Company Accounting Reform and Investor Protection Act, which was signed into law on July 31, 2002. Today this law is known as the Sarbanes-Oxley Act of 2002, after its principal sponsors, Paul S. Sarbanes and Michael G. Oxley. Sarbanes, a Democratic Senator from Maryland, was at the time the Chairman of the Senate Banking, Housing and Urban Affairs Committee. Oxley, a Republican Representative from Ohio, was then serving as the Chairman of the House Committee for Financial Services. Of possible interest is the fact that Sarbanes was the 2003 recipient of the Paul H. Douglas Ethics in Government Award from the University of Illinois,[4] and Oxley had retired from the FBI, and was a continuing member of Rotary International.[5]

The Sarbanes-Oxley Act was created in response to major scandals that came to light in 2001, most notably the failure of Enron Corporation, which was at the time one of the largest corporations in the United States. This law created an Accounting Control Board to oversee the accounting, internal controls and the outside auditors of publicly traded corporations. Among other provisions, the Act requires both the Chief Executive Officer and the Chief Financial Officer to certify the financial statements of their company, and face criminal penalties and financial sanctions if they knowingly sign false or misleading financial state-ments. Further, Sarbanes-Oxley bars the external auditors of public companies from engaging in non-audit services related to financial and securities processes of the company, such as information systems. This provision has resulted in many consulting division spin-offs from the major accounting firms. Companies are now required to have an internal ethics board, to disclose their code of ethics in their annual report, and to provide a statement of the effectiveness, truthfulness and accuracy of their internal control procedures.

We should not be surprised that this spate of scandals arose in the time frame of the year 2000, which was the era of the bursting of the "dot-com" bubble in the stock market. Why? Our economic leaders have been slow to focus on the need for integrity and self-regulation as characteristic of a healthy free market system. Even business schools have not addressed this need effectively. One of our read-ers articulated this very situation in the following question.

> Dear Jim:
>
> On May 20, 2003, *The New York Times* writes that according to a sur-vey of students, ethics is lacking in the business school curriculum. If the business schools of our country are not bringing this subject to the atten-tion of future leaders in effective ways, how much at risk is the free mar-ket system and its leadership?

Response:

> Free markets are at no greater risk simply because business schools do not adequately teach ethics in their classrooms. Free markets are not fun-damentally stronger because a higher percentage of students attending business schools are more eager to learn ways they can now articulate integrity-centered insights that might blunt unethical behavior. Free markets are designed to "self-correct" around customer needs, techno-logical breakthroughs, social changes and investor confidence levels. With or without the support of business schools, intelligent and moti-vated participants in free markets will respond to the expectations and demands of customers. The buying public is fed up with manipulations and lies. Perceptive business leaders will not ignore these important economic signals and expect to retain viability, and neither will for-ward-looking business professors who need to attract talented and thoughtful students.
>
> One of my mentors reminded me that we learn about things from books, and about people from other people. We can be taught from a

textbook about science, engineering, transportation and a host of other enterprises and activities. However, leadership, values, integrity-centered behavior, relationships and service—these are communicated and taught by those who exhibit them—person to person.

With reference to exhibiting integrity in leadership, and the origins of these values, there are scholars in the study of human behavior who suggest that fundamentals of character habits are well established before an individual is five years old. Even if these sociologists and psychologists are off by a few years, the implications are profound. What this means about shaping the moral values and standards of tomorrow's leaders is that our graduate business schools are quite late in the lives of their students in being able to provide much dramatic change, for the better or worse. Professors of business can guide and inspire, inform and direct, and leave students with legitimate models for effective and ethical economic structures. There is no doubt that free markets need wise and moral business instructors.

However, if the premise is accurate that one learns values from others and not textbooks (namely, from those engaged in the management of institutions), then professors of business and management can do little more than cite important and provocative examples, unless they happen to be actively engaged in leading an enterprise themselves. There comes a time in education when case studies need to be fortified (if not replaced) by face-to-face interaction with active integrity-centered leaders who can demonstrate appropriate behavior and the ramifications for both hitting and missing the mark. Creating a give-and-take academic environment, with educators seeking input from entrepreneurs, can enhance educational impact and restore the ethical to the practical. Business leaders need business instructors.

Successful learning generally happens best when need meets preparedness in the context of relationship and credibility. Few traditional classrooms can rally all four dimensions at the same time. Yet, when a motivated student asks important questions of a trusted and experienced individual, life-changing events are likely to unfold. When students, representing the future leadership of our society, encounter those whose lives and livelihood are successfully created by their own leadership of free markets, then we have an opportunity to strengthen values, in business and beyond.

Free markets are not doomed so long as those of the current leadership generation (business and academic) are preparing the next generation to listen to the buying public and evaluate all decisions in order to maintain a proper balance between self- interest and social responsibility.

This balance of self-interest and social responsibility was certainly not present during the decision processes that led to the previously mentioned scandals at Enron, WorldCom and Adelphia, which then led to the creation and passage of the Sarbanes-Oxley Act. Few people would argue with the *intent* of that Act, but it has forced immediate and wholesale changes in corporate management, which costs a good deal of money (which will be paid for ultimately by the public). The Act has had the effect of making highly qualified individuals reluctant to serve on corporate boards. The eventual effects are unknown today, but clearly this law is a representative of legislative response to public concern. The economic pendulum seems to swing from the behavioral excess of deteriorating values to restrictive legislation in response. Clearly, unless free markets regulate themselves, governments will.

NOTES

1   Lincoln used this phrase when accepting the Republican nomination for U.S. Senate from Illinois in June of 1858.

2   From a historical marker in Kiowa, Kansas: "Carry A. Nation, the militant crusader against illegal saloons, launched her career of saloon smashing in Kiowa. She and her followers in Medicine Lodge, her hometown, had closed the local saloons by holding prayer meetings on their premises and displays of force. However, as the Women's Christian Temperance Unions jail evangelist, she found as many drunks as ever in the county jail. These men named Kiowa as their source of supply. A voice spoke to Carry, telling her to go to Kiowa and smash the saloons. On June 1, 1900, she attacked three 'joints' in Kiowa, using stones, brickbats, full malt bottles, and one billiard ball as ammunition. Carry's attack surprised local officials, but because of the fact that the operation of such 'joints' was illegal she was not jailed, as she would be later in other communities. She did not adopt the use of her now famous hatchet until her visit to Wichita some six months later.

The Kiowa attack quickly received national attention and instigated great debate even among the temperance organizations. Carry Nation spent the remainder of her life in the crusade against the liquor interests and lecturing on prohibition. She died June 9, 1911."

3   As far back as the 13th century, officials in England (e.g., King Edward I) required the licensing of stockbrokers in the City of London.

4   The Paul H. Douglas Ethics in Government Award was created by the University of Illinois to honor the late Senator Paul H. Douglas of Illinois, who served during the years 1948 up to 1967, and was often referred to as "The conscience of the United States Senate."

5   Rotary International is a service organization whose members subscribe to a four-point code: 1) Is it the truth? 2) Is it fair to everyone concerned? 3) Will it build goodwill and better friendships? 4) Will it be beneficial to all concerned?

Chapter 3

Rebuilding from the Present

Because we are the land of the new beginning, we have a
special responsibility to aim true–so let us begin!
– Dan Halloran

Our society cannot improve if its individual citizens choose not to. For too long we have built an excuse-oriented society, each layer of excuse providing a platform for the next as we slide away from accountability. Parents refuse to tolerate a failing grade, but rather than accept that the responsibility likely falls on their child's performance, blame the teacher (frequently adding accusations of favoritism or incompetence). When an accident happens, there is a tendency to sue, because the fault couldn't possibly be due to individual clumsiness—it had to be the fault of the designer, the contractor, the floor-sweeper or some-one—anyone—else. No-fault insurance is a by-product of a culture without individual accountability.

A mentor of ours highlighted this problem with a wonderful and incisive story. This man was traveling in Norway, and approaching an office building in the rain, he noted to his Norwegian guide that the stairs looked very slippery, and inquired if there were not a safer way into the building. When the Norwegian companion responded, "No, this is the way into the building," our mentor replied, "Aren't you afraid of being sued?" "Well, in Norway," came the response, "we are responsible for where we put our feet!"

It should be obvious that individuals put society at risk when they demand that someone else accept responsibility for where they put their feet (or engage in self-indulgent and dysfunctional behavior). However, the opposite is also true. Society is strengthened when individuals accept responsibility and engage in interdependent, responsible behavior. The way forward involves looking for and acting upon opportunities for self-improvement, beginning with accountability in all transactions and relationships. It can be done.

In the early 1980's, manufacturing in the United States had become known for compromising quality, especially in comparison with the products (especially automobiles) manufactured in Japan and Germany. Competitive advantage seemed to have moved beyond the borders of the United States. Thoughtful leaders were concerned. However, the awakening to the need for improved quality often emerged one voice at a time (led by pioneer W. Edwards Demming). We assume that the changes started when an individual, somewhere, said to his or her fellow workers, "Enough!" And thus began the process of restoring a quality culture to manufacturing that led to The Malcolm Baldrige National Quality Award process as its premier focus. A national cultural change in manufacturing had begun. It took about a dozen years, but the point is that it happened!

To begin the process of renewal, then, requires steps to be taken, first by an individual, then by several individuals, and then organizations and companies. This is not "rocket science;" it is hard work. And it begins one step at a time.

Restoring integrity, similar to the quality movement, will require individual champions to lead the way. Every person reading this book is invited to become such an advocate. Depending on where the reader is on life's path, that person can strengthen integrity-centered leadership. One way to identify a point of entry could be the examination of each of the six roles outlined (and defined with the corresponding appropriate, effective behavior) below.

Parents and families (to provide unconditional love and acceptance, while nurturing socially responsive values): From birth, the individual grasps the fact of existence by relating with parents, and gradually the family. Infants, at birth, are capable of gross motion of arms and legs; the newborn can certainly make noise—indiscriminately. The very young are quick learners, observing their parents and their environment closely. They "connect the dots," as we say, very rapidly. They learn that their sounds bring a hug, food or fresh clothing; that a smile and giggle bring reciprocal encouragement from parents and caregivers.

Throughout childhood, the individual is taught a great deal from the behavior of the parents, who have an awesome responsibility and opportunity to shape the character of their young. From the accepting parent the child learns unconditional love; cause and effect; the value of pleasing others; self-discipline and consistency.

The character of the child is formed as he or she learns the value of truth, of full disclosure, of authority and of fulfilling obligations, or what we call "partnership." The child also observes that rewards go with performance, and that failure is sometimes unpleasant. The child also comprehends generosity and graciousness as awareness of the rights of other people become apparent and are respected. We all know this, intuitively.

Parents who become aware that everything they say, the manner in which it is said, everything that they do, and the competence with which it is done, are more effective in their integrity-centered parenting for their observing child. Parents need to realize that they are "onstage," to one degree or another, for their children all the time; they are demonstrating the art of life—and living—to their children. Some examples are appropriate:

1. Parents can speak to spouses and other family members with respect. A whispered kindness between parents, when witnessed by the young observer, may bring reassurance and comfort;

2. Adults who look for opportunities to help one another in the home teach children to do likewise;

3. Children learn the value of time as they observe their parents being punctual and as they listen to parents encourage them to be responsive to commitments;

4. Adults act as role models when teaching younger people how to do things properly, helping them to learn from their mistakes and recognizing them for their achievements;

5. The young observe another form of integrity when their parents speak well of neighbors and decline to spread gossip;

6. Respect for the law, for rules and discipline, is communicated when parents obey traffic signs and regulations;

7. Children learn to take care of things and to put things away when that is the condition seen in the home, and in the behavior of family members;

8. The value of continuous education is taught when young eyes and ears observe parents enjoying a good book, or when discussions at the dinner table focus on important ideas and events.

We know, of course, the other side: the abusive parent, the lazy oaf, the constant critic, the reckless driver, the gossip, the slob. The following column speaks to an incident of parental failure, yet also discloses how another parent might use an event as a teaching opportunity.

Dear Jim:

My daughter came home with a story that is appalling to me. Her friend in her English class at our local high school turned in a paper on the Supreme Court and received the only "A" in the class. When I told my daughter, "That's wonderful," she quickly took issue, and said that her friend's mother actually wrote it for her daughter, because the girl was behind, frantic, and besides, the girl knew her mother would do it for her.

Jim, what chance does that girl have, if she always finds someone to do her work for her? Where is our country's future if the young children of today are taught that this form of parental fraud is ok?

Response:

This is a disappointing story. Assuming your daughter has the facts accurately, then we are looking at lying, cheating, stealing and negligence. Your daughter's friend has a mother who has abdicated leadership responsibilities as a parent and citizen. Your daughter's friend has been taught that cheating is OK in order to win; some other child has likely been denied the recognition of having created the best paper. This is simply an awful representation of gross negligence of parental responsibility.

The daughter is being taught by this example to lie to people in positions of responsibility in order to achieve recognition. She now knows how to avoid commitments. She is being shown how to cheat the system in order to win, and worse, is being assisted in the fraud by her own mother. Parental negligence is apparent; this young woman is at risk in lots of ways.

Parental responsibilities include teaching accountability. Poor school habits have long-term negative consequences, and should not be replaced by parental interference. Instead of holding her daughter accountable, this selfish and shortsighted mother is passing along the dishonesty that is eating away at our society. This daughter has been enabled to betray her responsibility to learn and to perform. She has broken her trust with her teacher. And, her very own mother is helping her to run even further from responsibility. This mother and daughter need help.

However, you can turn this into a learning experience for your own daughter, using it as a way to put across the values that you obviously hold, of honesty, accountability and character. Consider asking your daughter to think through whether she should be associating herself with so-called friends who lack the integrity to do their own work, and ask her whether her cheating friend could be counted upon to be honorable in defense of her friends? Would she ever again trust this girl when she might be saying, "I did this?" Let us hope that the larger share of your daughter's friends hold to a higher standard than represented by this story; and you make sure to use this episode as a way to help your daughter appreciate the value of integrity.

Without the keystone of integrity beginning within the family, the structures of our society are at risk. In this particular set of circumstances, there is a real issue for this family, the individuals who know this story, and the people touched by this young woman in the future. Were this story about drug abuse, involving a parent purchasing and sharing illegal drugs with an under-age family member, one would know immediately which laws were being broken. However, the heady stuff of false achievement introduced by the mother's fraudulent actions beg for discovery, and soon.

Here is the good news: if you explain why you would never sanction such plagiarism, your daughter will have been taught solid values, learned to appreciate the consequences of dishonest behavior, and see you in the light of integrity-centered parenting. Remember, integrity matters, all of the time.

If a better society is to be built, the focus must be on what can be done better, starting first within the family, and then within society as a whole.

Educators (to enable learning for all who seek to grow their minds), one of whom was a victim of the term-paper fraud described above, also frequently share the role as parents themselves, and have a special and unique opportunity to help rebuild our society. Because they are specifically charged with the responsibility to teach children in specific subject areas, educators have the platform to communicate a great deal—both about the designated subject, and about other subjects they might deem appropriate. Educators can help build a better society, first, by executing their responsibilities well (i.e., preparation, organization and skill in presentation).

Approachable teachers are viewed by some students as a third party to whom they can go for advice. Society has a term, "in loco parentis," meaning that during the school day, the educator stands in place of the parents—at least in primary and secondary schools. Accordingly, educators have the responsibility to be careful and caring in the execution of their student relationships. Through parent-teacher conferences the educator can better understand the student's personal environment; the teacher has the additional opportunity to impact the life of the student beyond the classroom.

Spiritual leaders (to exhibit and live their messages) bear a similar responsibility to educators and families: to be role models as they coach and counsel their followers with a defined set of values. Spiritual representatives would appear to occupy a lonely position as moral guides, living with their own humanity on display along with every nuance of their imperfections open to criticism. However, their integrity resides squarely upon how they exhibit and live their messages. Recently, news reports of lapses of moral courage on the part of some religious authorities have stunned believers. The "Integrity Matters" response to the following question during the recent pedophile scandal can provide perspective in this area.

Dear Jim:

I am a Catholic who feels betrayed by the behavior of the Catholic Church, most typified by Cardinal Law in Boston. Even though he has resigned, I am left feeling that [the] integrity of my Faith remains damaged. What can the Catholic Church, or Cardinal Law, or even I, do to repair the damage and begin to rebuild the trust?

Response:

The current mess in the Roman Catholic Church is awful. Some small percentage of the clergy has broken laws. Whether they have broken moral, civil or criminal laws is for someone else to judge.

Regardless of titles or tasks, whether in business or religion, leaders who break the rules of relationships, violating trust, put at risk their organization's future.

With reference to your own course of action, please consider this:

1. Institutions (business, government, religion) are bigger than any fraction of irresponsible individuals;

2. Learning from mistakes (big or small) is the key for growth and renewal. Most of us have learned more from failure than from success;

3. People in power who hide behind laws and precedents prolong their own pain, and fail to capture the real moment for meaning. They withdraw from learning and minimize the possibility for a constructive legacy; and,

4. For you, the response seems clear: maintain your values and support the institution you love.

Elected and appointed employees of the government (to transcend self-serving goals and truly serve all of the people) hold positions of public trust by supporting the common good. They oversee security, safety, health, justice, transportation, and are responsible for providing a level playing field for our free market system. When performed efficiently and effectively, there is no greater calling than public service. For the most part, citizens trust that water will be drinkable, modes of transportation will be available, medicines will be safe, mail will be delivered, cars will be registered, and taxes will be collected and distributed appropriately.

Yet, questions do arise, and some citizens worry. Corporate scandals have had their negative effect, generating anxiety among the public about the prosecution of those accused of crimes. Some portion of tax dollars is set aside to protect the public from harm, globally and domestically, from terrorists to white-collar criminals. At the point when confidence in the effectiveness of government systems is shaken, people can lose their desire to participate in the democratic processes, which can range from voting to paying taxes. When partisan politics replaces commitment to the common good, where integrity-centered governmental leadership is compromised, our free market democracy is at risk. One such concern emerges from the following question.

> Dear Jim:
>
> What next? *The Dallas Morning News* announces that "Two Top Enron Executives Escape Indictment." Where is justice? What happened to integrity? Who can we trust? Can we still have confidence in business and government? Jeffrey Skilling continues to spend time with his family and Ken Lay is now working at a business start-up. These are the two men who oversaw the highflying Enron Corporation and they are denying accountability for the billions squandered. Neither of them faces any criminal charges. To make matters even worse, the Justice Department pronounces itself "very satisfied" with the work of its Enron Task Force. This task force has secured indictments of 19 former executives. Is this a justice system with integrity?

> Response:
>
> You asked several questions. The last one asks about the integrity of the justice system. In a word, the answer is YES, there is integrity in our system. Were it not the case, questions like yours and columns like mine would never be in print. We do have freedom of the press in the United States and we can ask hard questions, openly.

Take heart, it is not over for Skilling and Lay, at least, not yet. Apart from headlines, the investigation continues. Many students of the law who are observers of the Enron mess believe that criminal charges may yet be filed against one or both of these individuals, and relatively soon. If you are frustrated by the very slow pace of the investigation, you are not alone. The eight or nine federal prosecutors who make up the task force of the Justice Department have been assisted by about 30 agents of the Federal Bureau of Investigation. They have been working on this case since January 2002. These kinds of investigations are complicated and take time.

Progress is being made: Andrew Fastow, Enron's former Chief Financial Officer, faces 99 counts ranging from obstruction of justice to money laundering. Also, a result of this investigative process, Enron's auditor, Arthur Andersen, was found guilty in a June 2002, in a jury trial of obstruction of justice.

There are reports that Mr. Lay, 61, loomed large in Houston philanthropic circles and was a top contributor to President Bush's 2000 campaign. Both Skilling and Lay maintain that they knew nothing about the fraud of Enron.

If there was fraud, and there is little evidence to deny gross mismanagement, perhaps criminal intent, by those leading Enron, and still they say that they knew nothing about it, then their board should have fired them for incompetence. If they did have knowledge and are lying, then the justice system can address appropriate penalties. If the leaders knew, and the members of the board knew, and no one blew the whistle, then our federal prisons systems may consider building lots more cells.

So very much of what makes our country "tick" revolves around uncomplicated behaviors: we make promises and we keep them. We go the extra mile when necessary and we support one another in hard times. We enjoy success and we avoid excess. We value employees and serve customers. Leaders own the defeats and failures and pass along to others the credit for victories.

When these unwritten rules of management and labor integrity are broken, our system of checks and balances will rise up to make things right. Integrity-centered responsibility reminds each and every participant in the free market system that we must maintain the proper balance between legitimate self-interest and social responsibility. Destructive and self-serving greed must be regulated.

Community involvement, the dues we pay for the privileges of economic and personal fulfillment, must be encouraged. When our system misses the mark and does not live up to its promises for every citizen, then we must stand up and be counted. Phrases like "whistleblowers" and "snitches" need to be replaced with more appropriate and noble terms like "character coaches" and "mentors of the free market"—for the magic of renewing our society rests with how we accept important and inevitable input, even when it is critical. We must be willing to hear the evil, see the evil and then make it better.

And so the value of the government employee, elected or appointed, who performs diligently and effectively is underscored visibly in high-profile legal cases that have characteristics of extreme public interest. How the justice system handles the crimes of the rich and powerful will shape the confidence and trust of the public.

Celebrities and public figures (to model admirable behaviors, including appreciation, humility and self-discipline): In a 1993 Nike television commercial, a professional basketball player named Charles Barkley solemnly warned the audience, "I am not a role model. Parents should be role models." Of course, we agree with the second part of Barkley's statement—parents do need to be the role models for their children; that is one of their most important responsibilities. As children become aware of the world outside of the family (particularly in adolescence), the surrounding environment becomes increasingly important, and they learn from their peers, from their heroes and from celebrities. Preteens and teens have a strong tendency to identify with those individuals in society who have achieved celebrity through their specific talents, often in sports or the performing arts. It is not integrity-centered behavior for these privileged, powerful and wealthy individuals to profess, as Barkley did, that they are not role models. By the attention their celebrity generates, they are role models who will be imitated. They cannot escape it. Celebrities and public figures must model admirable behaviors, including appreciation, humility and self-discipline.

Children watch their star athletes and artists perform, and admire their talent, their skill and their execution. Fans observe what their heroes do away from their particular area of expertise. If a sports hero or a popular actress/actor says to "Drive a Buick," then there may be a positive impact on the sale of Buicks. That is precisely why sponsoring companies are so willing to pay significant royalties to these "heroes." They are role models. They impact behavior.

As a consequence, public figures have the responsibility to live their lives with respect for the law, discretion in speech, and self-control. The following column describes a loss of self-control by celebrity sports figures, and the public damage that such behavior represents.

Dear Jim:

The newspaper today had an article in the sports section which described how Winston Cup driver Jimmy Spencer rear-ended fellow driver Kurt Busch at the Michigan International Speedway in pit row after the race and then got out of his race car, ran to Busch's car, reached in and punched Busch several times before being restrained. Busch reportedly has a broken nose. One or more other drivers were said to have supported Jimmy Spencer, which seems to reward irresponsible behavior. What does this say about the integrity of this sport?

Response:

First, one person losing his temper is not saying anything negative about an entire sport. Two individuals were engaged in an altercation. Yes, immature behavior does say something about those who are engaged in it. These two world-class race car drivers, Busch and Spencer, have had run-ins on the track in the past. In March 2002, at Bristol Motor Speedway, Busch bumped past Spencer to get his first Winston Cup victory. There have been several on-course incidents since, but not physical confrontations.

Allowing competitive frustrations to boil over into violent acts defeats the purpose of sports competition. Once upon a time, sports were viewed as the socially acceptable way for warring factions, even ancient cities, to work out their frustrations with one another. Bragging rights on the sports field replaced dead bodies on the battlefield. We hope our progress in the past continues and does not regress in to random acts of violence, road rage being but one example.

Second, having attended a NASCAR race, the Brickyard 400 at Indianapolis, it is incredible that more bumps don't become catastrophes. Lots of money is at stake for each finishing position, to say nothing of the points earned for standings in the annual championship race. Points mean dollars, millions and millions of them. Being pushed out of contention, inappropriately, is serious business. These automobiles move like rockets with wheels, only inches from one another, sometimes three across into skidding turns. Competition is fierce. The physical and mental stresses must be overwhelming. Any mistake or miscalculation can risk significant rewards, even life itself. This is not simply a game; it is the livelihood, perhaps even the life, of those capable of handling the competition.

Third, is this the end of the "race-track" feud? Will it now escalate until someone is seriously injured or killed? Cheap shots and cheating in any part of life, including sports, violate the integrity of creating a level playing field. When lethal weapons in a driver's hands, in the form of pieces of steel capable to moving nearly 200 miles per hour, are directed at doing harm, disaster cannot be far behind.

Fifty-four years ago, a neighbor, also four years old at the time, joined me to watch my father build a fence. Dad was busy digging holes, placing posts in the ground and nailing boards. For some reason the little fellow, Jimmy, decided to see if the hammer my father had be using would reshape the back of my skull. It did. My scream alerted Dad that all was not well. Blood streaming down my face was a problem. As he carried me toward the car, on the way to the hospital, the mother of the little Jimmy "hammer slammer" was heard asking in a loud voice, "Who hit first?" Both of my parents told me many years later that they had been horrified with the response.

It did not last for a long time, but little Jimmy and I did not play together for a while. And when we did, things were back to normal, except for the bump on my head. Even so, it was never appropriate for me to retaliate. Nor did my parents carry a grudge. Rather, the incident in our family was a lesson in manners, graciousness and care for those about us: both parents and children. Misjudgments happen. Young people and adults make mistakes. Situations find remedies. And, so too should the folks at NASCAR. We are taught that two wrongs do not make a right. Integrity matters.

Bosses (to build a healthy environment for productivity) make knowledge practical by expanding the role of teacher from the educators and parents once an individual enters the workforce. Bosses are in a position to teach accountability and responsibility. They instruct in techniques and introduce the "rules of the game," which include the policies and folklore of the working culture. From around ages 18–21 until retirement, bosses of one kind or another influence the individual via his or her work environment. Vision comes from the organization's leader. Leaders, through words and consistent actions, make the mission of the company achievable. Responsible leaders make the goals and objectives clear in order to build a healthy environment for productivity.

Leaders of organizations have a responsibility to engage in integrity-centered practices. The purpose of most enterprises is to serve customer needs, effectively, efficiently and profitably. Creating a productive environment that focuses on the customer requires that bosses understand interpersonal communications, goal-setting and individual needs—of customers, employees and colleagues. Business leaders can therefore impact the overall health, direction and growth of our society in significant ways. Business—not government—is the economic engine of our society. Therefore business leaders have a key role in restoring trust in the free market system and the various institutions upon which society depends.

The following question from an "Integrity Matters" reader, along with its response, provides a summary of what type of behavior we should expect from our business leaders.

> Dear Jim:
>
> Mr. Grasso is history, at least as far as the New York Stock Exchange is concerned. While Mr. Grasso may be guilty of helping design an overly generous compensation program for himself at the expense of his member companies (and therefore widows, orphans and pension funds), the real culprits are the directors of the NYSE who approved the plans. These directors clearly failed to do their job. How would you describe a good director for a good board at a good company?

> Response:
>
> You have asked for answers to three questions, about what makes for a good director, a good board and a good company. The answers involve integrity-centered leadership behaviors.
>
> First, we look at good directors. They are effective based upon their insight, impact and integrity. Good directors understand the company (its products, services, markets and financial health); respond to the needs of all stakeholders; and exhibit courage, even in the face of strong opposition.
>
> Good directors work hard to understand the enterprise and management that they have been asked to guide. Directors hire and fire chief executives and set their pay packages. They earn their own salaries by preparing for and responsibly attending their board and committee

meetings. Good directors are committed to the effectiveness of their involvement. They wrestle hard issues to the ground and do not rest until proper resolution has been attained. Good directors seldom plead ignorance. They do exhibit courage.

Let us look at some recent high-profile scandals. In the Enron debacle, the outside directors didn't dig deeply enough to understand and question the complex financial structures that were created and the risks associated with them. In the case of the NYSE there may have been an integrity issue since many of the board members were employed by the very companies that they, the NYSE and Mr. Grasso, were charged with regulating. In the cases of WorldCom and Tyco the directors apparently knew about the loans to Ebbers [WorldCom's former Chief Executive Officer] and excesses by Kozlowski [Tyco's Chief Executive Officer] but did not courageously confront something they knew was wrong. In the case of the insider investigation against Martha Stewart, the allegations suggest that integrity was ignored in favor of greed.

What is so striking about these headline cases suggesting impropriety, misbehavior or malfeasance is the similarity of the creeping scandalous behavior to the description of the five progressive stages of intoxication:

- stage one, after several drinks, the drinker becomes clever;

- stage two, a couple of more drinks, the drinker becomes charming and affectionate;

- stage three, as alcoholic consumption continues, the drinker believes that no one can see their clumsy behaviors or notice the slurring of words;

- stage four the alcohol level rises, and the partaker is now convinced of their own invincibility and immunity to rules that apply to others;

- stage five, the lights begin to go out and the behavior spirals out of control.

The substance abuser may well end up in a cell doing time, either because of actual harm caused to others, or because of the violation of public drunkenness laws.

We have seen one small step of greed or power after another leading to the scandals that parallel intoxication. This demonstrates that power may insidiously corrupt those who attain it. And again, with the

Sarbanes-Oxley Act, we see that unless individuals and institutions regulate themselves, governments will.

A good director, then, is that person whose character, values, insight and knowledge create positive and purposeful influence with colleagues on the board.

On the subject of a good board, these exhibit and encourage independence, interdependence, directness (confrontation) and relationships built upon mutual trust and respect. Seventy-five percent of the board members should be outsiders. No board member should be so captivated by the organization's influence, or that of suppliers or customers, that alignment with the needs of shareholders and other stakeholders is compromised. Good boards want and need oversight, never to be rubber stamps for powerful executives and their teams. This professional independence does not mean that a bank's board member might not have a small account at the bank, or that a board member of General Electric might not have been using GE light bulbs or watching NBC television stations. Nor does this independence require an adversarial board atmosphere. Independence simply means providing the environment for confronting issues openly and honestly, all the time.

Interdependence is also a hallmark of good boards. Being a strategic partner with management is important. Company managements need the strategic insights, ideas, experience and referrals that a good, yet diverse, board can provide. To be a source of ideas, which a good board is, the relationships must provide for responsible give and take.

Good boards attract and retain individuals who are able to get along, enjoy one another, even in the midst of strongly differing positions, sustain substantive relationships built upon mutual respect and trust. Good boards communicate their own healthy culture of integrity that includes how they work together, through tough issues, in a climate that combines fiduciary responsibility and stakeholder sensitivity. Good boards insist upon adherence to the mission of the enterprise, as it is fulfilled in all activities of the organization.

The diversity of good boards enables creativity, connections, cultural and market insight, advice and counsel. Similarly, good boards are not afraid to tackle tough issues, openly. Debate, which implies differing positions, is essential, not optional. It is important to remember that our college and university students are being taught by their professors and from their textbooks that "the board of directors is a group of elected individuals whose primary responsibility is to act in the owners' interests by formally monitoring and controlling the corporation's top-level executives." (*Strategic Management*, 2003, p. 319; by Hitt, Ireland and Hoskinson)

The third question, that of a good company is answered as one that does what it says it will do, and tells the truth about what it does, seven days a week and fifty-two weeks a year. The good company is integrity-centered and exhibits behaviors that enable its stakeholders to answer "yes" to the questions that reflect the Eight Attributes of an integrity-centered company developed by the Bracher Center.

1. **CHARACTER: Consistency Between Word and Deed**
   - Do the leaders of your organization exhibit congruence between what they say and what they do, as well as what they say about what they did?

2. **HONESTY: Truthful Communication**
   - Do you have confidence that your leaders would never engage in or sanction misrepresentation?

3. **OPENNESS: Operational Transparency**
   - Is appropriate information about your organization readily available?

4. **AUTHORITY: Employee Encouragement**
   - Are you able to correct a customer problem? Do you have confidence that your actions will be supported?

5. **PARTNERSHIP: Honor Obligations**
   - Does your organization pride itself on the timely fulfillment of all commitments?

6. **PERFORMANCE: Accountability Throughout the Organization**
   - If individuals, including senior executives, underperform repeatedly, are they given due process and then, if necessary, replaced?

7. **CHARITY: Generous Community Stewardship**
   - Does your organization reach out to those in need?

8. **GRACIOUSNESS: Respect and Discipline**
   - Does your organization demonstrate care and concern for all stakeholders?

When you find an organization, a good company, that exhibits these attributes, there is a good chance, quite probable in fact, that they will have a good board and good directors.

Self-regulation communicates discipline and accountability, important building blocks for integrity-centered leadership. To move beyond individual impact and create social improvement, certain behaviors must be exhibited. The following pages examine the Eight Attributes and clarify actions taken by people we might emulate in the trust-restoring journey for our society. The attributes serve as touchstones for the next eight chapters as we guide the integrity-centered conversation toward the renewal of confidence in leadership. As a mentor of ours was fond of saying, "Do the right thing now...Do it...Do it right...Do it now."

Chapter 4

CHARACTER: Consistency Between Word and Deed

Your organization's behavior is the world's window
on you and your values.
— Jim Bracher

The self-regulation of free markets begins with individuals and requires strength of character. Individuals are said to have character when they can be consistently depended upon to respond in support of others; when they have the courage to stand firm on principle; and when they model to others the common sense, grace and humility that earn respect, in support of their spoken values. These people display actions that inform the world about the integrity of their character. Just as individuals are judged primarily by their actions, we know that an organization's leadership behavior is the world's window on its character. There are many definitions of "integrity of character." We define it as consistency between what you say and what you do, as well as what you say about what you did. Integrity is the keystone of leadership. Character is the foundation of integrity.

Companies can, and do, use the words "integrity" or "character" in their advertising. Transactions and the products themselves are so described. Management can be said to have it, and employees often behave with integrity, or show great character. This chapter is concerned with the behaviors that speak to, or suggest the absence of, the integrity of character.

Character issues may arise outside the context of work. Sometimes these challenges bring along painful lessons, especially when friendship is involved. The following column demonstrates that not everyone lives the same values.

Dear Jim:

About 15 months ago, I was winding down from a set of tennis over drinks with one of my best friends. As we were talking, I suddenly had an idea for what I thought was a clever new product concept. When I told my friend the idea he smiled and said something like, "Yeah, that would be great." The idea drifted out of my consciousness almost immediately, as I assumed it had for my friend.

Last week I was catching up on neighborhood happenings with my wife. She casually informed me that my friend's wife told her that her husband has just sold his rights in a new product to a big company with nationwide distribution. As it turns out my "best friend" had developed my idea – designs, patents, copyrights, etc. – and then cashed in on it. When I confronted the friend he said that he didn't really think I was that serious about my idea and that it wasn't until months after I told him the concept that he thought it might be worth pursuing.

I was devastated. I probably don't have any legal rights to my idea, but it's not the money part of this that's plaguing me. There has been an integrity break with my longtime friend that is irreconcilable. Yet, our wives and kids are inseparable. How can I be true to myself, and at the same time minimize the impact of my issues on others?

Response:

Your concerns are understandable. Your friendship has been tainted by what you feel has been a breach of trust, honesty and possibly some of your own naiveté. So, how do you minimize the impact of this disappointment, not only for you and your buddy, but also upon your families?

There are three relationship "checks" that could minimize damages to your friendships:

1. Assuming that you will not elect to call together the other friends who gathered with you after the tennis match many months ago and ask them to "reconstruct" the conversations regarding the source of the idea; and assuming that you have no desire to participate in any kind of legal action, then you are completely clear that the issue is really more about the friendship than the dollars. If you pursue any legal recourse, the consequences to the relationships may be serious. Make your decision and don't look back.

2. Find an opportunity to clarify with your friend the nature and depth of your concern. There is always the possibility that you mis-communicated the seriousness of your business idea and your desire to solicit feedback about its viability prior to your own implementation. Regardless of how this conversation turns out, you will have learned ways to improve

the clarity of your own communication, the receptivity of your friend to share ownership for the "foul-up" in your relationship, and more effective ways to discuss proprietary information, even among friends.

3. Remember: Integrity is congruence between what you say and what you do, as well as what you say about what you did. If you avoid legal confrontation and find a shared ownership for the problem, then the relationship can emerge even stronger than before. You own some of the responsibility because you discussed a business idea without fully disclosing that you intended to make it your own.

This may have been an expensive lesson. What was or is at risk are money, friendship and family relationships. Count the costs and learn from the experience.

It is very important in our relationships that we are clear about expectations. Further, we must be careful about the assumptions we make and the actions we take. A small vignette may clarify this. A man with a history of staying out late, bowling and drinking with his friends and generally ignoring his family, called home one night and told his spouse, "Dear, I have to work late tonight, and will not be home for dinner." To this his wife responded, "OK, dear, I'll see you when you get home!" A straightforward communication? Not really, for his wife heard his excuse through the memories of his past behavior, and assumed that he was going out with his friends, drinking, again. For his part, the man had a long history of being able to stay out without recriminations, so heard his wife to be acknowledging his work issue. In truth, she was angry, and had meant that she would deal with him when he got home. Since he truly had to work late, he was confounded by seeing the angry spouse who greeted him upon his arrival.

Turning to the workplace, employees discover the character of their leaders by observing their behavior. They also learn what is important, what is relevant and what is unnecessary, in order to be successful. As baseball celebrity Yogi Berra says, "You can observe a lot by just watching." Below is an example that demonstrates the role that leaders—at any level—play in setting standards for their employees.

Dear Jim:

As managers, do we terminate an employee who we know committed sexual harassment? Do we fire the individual now or when the boss returns?

Response:

> Assuming the facts are clear, you need to do what is right ... immediately. Forget convenience and honor integrity. At least suspend the offender until the boss can finalize the release. If you are in a larger organization with a Human Resources department, you need to involve them immediately.
>
> To do otherwise, of course, would communicate both to other workers and to the world that harassment is tolerated. The cumulative effect of tolerating even subtle policy infractions can be disastrous to the character of an organization. If sexual innuendoes and inappropriate photos are tolerated, if badgering and sarcasm are accepted, then the potential harasser is given the message that his or her baser inclinations will be acceptable. It goes beyond harassment and extends to the paycheck as well. If a good worker receives the same recognition as the mediocre worker, the message becomes clear that mediocrity is acceptable, and that the character of the organization is weak. Productivity seldom goes up when there exists an erosion of confidence in the integrity of leadership.

Other behavior may imply that values are only important for the front-line employee. Certainly that is true of executive compensation, where we sometimes find executives "cutting a better deal" for themselves right in the middle of an economic retrenchment, displaying the character flaw of greed. The following two letters from our readers expose such behavior.

> Dear Jim:
>
> It is being discussed and written about seemingly everywhere: American CEO's, on average, this past year were paid 241 times as much as the average worker. This seems unfair and a violation of integrity. Am I right?

Response:

> Grossly overpaid executives are enabled to "take" all they can get by their very own boards of directors. Where they are being over-compensated, not only are they are taking money from their own employees, but also from the risk-taking investors who entrust them to create an appropriate return. However, like spoiled children who have just finished a well-balanced meal that had already included a wonderful dessert of large salary and bonus, stock options and retirement packages, these self-absorbed bosses are seeking even more. Just like ravenously undisciplined and

spoiled children screaming for more cake and ice cream, these unhealthy appetites cannot seem to be satisfied.

Are these compensation packages unfair? No, not if the results match the rewards. If the leadership of an organization enhances the productivity and profitability, then what is wrong with rewarding those who generated it? There is no integrity violation when individuals do what they are supposed to do and then are rewarded for it. The issue raised is that these lucrative "goodies" are not being distributed appropriately to sustain the motivation of all who helped create the successes. There needs to be a geometrically proportional link between what the boss receives and what others receive. That lack of an appropriate distribution is absolutely unfair. This is not about socialism's equal distribution; rather, it is about what causes workers and bosses to respect and appreciate one another, year after year, and still want to work together productively in the future.

Is the crazy high pay for mediocre or poor performance an integrity issue? Certainly it is. According to Holly Sklar's book, *Raise the Floor: Wages and Policies that Work for All of Us*, when CEO's are paid, on average, 241 times that of the average worker, then the boards of directors' levels of accountability should be evaluated. Obviously, sanctioning compensation inequities means that board members are not thinking and acting responsibly. They are failing to act on behalf of either their own investors or on behalf of the workforce upon which their enterprise depends.

Compensation committees can recommend any salary and benefits package they can dream up. However, when it is the board of directors that must approve these gigantic rewards, then they must do the work for which they are paid: ensure the viability of the enterprise and reward investors appropriately. Any other leadership approach by a board of directors would seem to border on the illegal and the irresponsible. Certainly, careless decision-making by boards resulting in outrageous CEO pay might cause investors to question their judgments in other areas. There is little doubt that rank-and-file employees have already concluded that such decisions are violating the integrity and trust that needs to exist between themselves and their organizations.

Because there is a need for guidance in areas of judgment and responsibility, it became apparent that someone ought to provide integrity-centered leadership counsel. Now that the Bracher Center has defined this area of service, we know that through our integrity-based services, we can improve productivity for the investor, executive, team, culture, organization and the individual. However, such productivity will be enhanced most effectively when all constituents and all stakeholders choose to regulate themselves. We are confident that free markets, often directed by boards of directors, must regulate themselves or governments will. Outrageous compensation is an integrity issue and must be addressed or we risk the viability of free enterprise itself.

In fact, as reported by the *U.S. Wall Street Journal*/Mercer CEO compensation survey (2002), the average CEO earned $1.8 million in combined salary and bonus, with long-term incentives making up 68 percent of their total compensation. A little math tells us that the average CEO received a total, then, of $5.625 million! The National Compensation Survey published in July 2003 by the U.S. Department of Labor for the year 2002 revealed that the average worker earned $17.12 per hour, for a derived total of $35,700 per year. The actual multiple of CEO pay was therefore 156 times the average worker—still an enormous gulf! When times are good, and senior management is generously rewarded, the issue may simply be an irritation to the employee, but may not rise above the level of coffee-break conversation. However, when such a company encounters economic reversal, the unjust enrichment of top management will encourage the best employees to look elsewhere, or lose heart, as the following discloses.

Dear Jim:

I'm in the human resources department for a high-tech company. Our business is way down, like most companies in our industry. Having lost 40 percent of our employees over the last two years has created a lot of wear and tear on me because I'm involved in outplacement. I really don't have any good news for the laid-off staff. There are no new jobs to be had in our area for most skills and it doesn't look like we'll be rehiring anytime soon.

But what's really bothering me is our senior management. They seem to be in denial. There's so much money being wasted. We still have our corporate jets, fancy perks and big expense accounts. There's also a rumor that the Chief Executive Officer (CEO) and Chief Operating Officer (COO) paid themselves substantial bonuses last year. I read about WorldCom and Enron and start to get really cynical. Are all companies run by greedy me-first people? I don't know if I can look one more co-worker in the eye as I hand them their severance check and try to explain why they are being laid off. On the other hand I find it tough to stand on the moral high ground when I feel so desperate to keep my own job so I can take care of my family.

Response:

You are not alone. You are not in control of the behaviors of others. Your integrity stands on its own. From the time history was recorded, bad things have happened to good people. Given your responsibilities to yourself, your family and your colleagues, pause and put together your own plan. If you cannot see integrity flickering in your leaders' eyes, engineer a plan for your own exit. You cannot represent integrity in an organization that has none. Balance your own desire to sustain your personal and organizational values while simultaneously remaining responsible for the health and welfare of those you love best.

Now, for the future. If nothing substantive changes where you are, you will probably move on. Establish the right criteria for responsible leadership. You can develop the list from what you see done poorly where you are and from what might also be done well. Build this list into a performance scorecard. Utilize the information in future interviews. Even painful learning is learning.

In summary:

1. Assess your own needs and those for whom you are responsible.

2. Determine what the right (sensible and prudent) time is to move on, but only after thoroughly addressing financial needs and future opportunities.

3. Seek leadership next time that more clearly fits with your definition of integrity in leadership.

4. Move on when you find the right situation.

Contracts of executives may contain evidence of their character, but not be visible externally (except for the very top executives in publicly owned companies). How, then, can you know whether a private company has integrity in this area? A strong clue comes from turnover. We all know that people are drawn to companies that have a reputation for integrity, and the turnover of management in such companies tends to be low. A symptom of a company that may have lost its way on the path of integrity is the rapid turnover of key management employees. Such leadership changes are often very visible. The following provides an illustration of this condition.

Dear Jim:

Why does it seem like a certain local, large hospitality organization, seemingly a fine company, can't keep management?

Response:

... Some facts never change. Quality leadership and integrity generally attract and retain the best people. The exception will prove the rule. There are always reasons why folks choose to change organizations, and that is another reason to live and work in the United States of America. We are free to do pretty much what we want.

Without responding to any company in particular, retention is generally all about leadership and values. Books are written about retaining employees. Seminars and training programs are offered to thousands and even millions of attendees annually, probably netting the providers incredible profits. But that approach may be missing the mark. Leadership effectiveness is uncomplicated. At least that is what we have learned during the past 24 years consulting with about 8,000 clients.

Most of our executive development and leadership enhancement consultation centers on training individuals with lots of responsibilities. They often need to learn to incorporate three important phrases that were taught to many of us who remember Bob Keeshan, whose television name was "Captain Kangaroo." The Captain was a pioneer in television programming, focused on children. He preceded Mr. Rogers and taught many of the same valuable insights. His three lessons could save management careers. His basic approach might catapult leaders (or "want to be leaders") if only they would learn to think, feel and say:

1. PLEASE
2. THANK YOU
3. I AM SORRY, I MADE A MISTAKE

Organizations that fail to emphasize these practical and profound behaviors risk losing a great deal, beginning with customers, employees and managers. Captain Kangaroo and Mr. Rogers taught integrity. We can profit from their wisdom.

These two gentlemen have demonstrated good character in their television efforts, contributing to the shaping the character of many in today's adult population. Fred Rogers was quoted as saying: "We have to remember to whom the airwaves belong, and we must put as great an emphasis on the nurturing of the human personality as we can." Today, any definition of the airwaves must also include the Internet. The emergence of the Internet and its "worldwide web" has created new opportunities to demonstrate integrity. The consistency between how a company presents itself on a Website and the reality of its corporate behavior can be relatively clear. The Web has also provided a new avenue for at least two common challenges: how to take care of personal business when working for an employer, and whether an employer should read an employee's mail. Both issues are addressed below.

> Dear Jim:
>
> My boss just called me on the carpet for sending an e-mail to purchase some blinds for my home. I could have taken time off to go to a nearby mall and do it, no problem, but with my workload, I thought it would be simpler to engage in the purchase on line. Fine, next time I'll take the hour or so to go shopping—but now I'm upset! They are reading my e-mail! Isn't that a violation of my right to privacy, my First Amendment rights, etc.?

Response:

> Whoa! Slow down. While private time when at work is a legal tangle that lies outside my expertise, common sense and some of my own personal business experiences might shed light on the problems you raise. Being "called on the carpet" for what amounts to your making a purchase with your office Internet connection may seem out of bounds, at least in terms of a solid working relationship. In my own business, when an employee is busy with personal activities when I need their help, once or twice, there is generally not a problem. However, when personal priorities become a frequent intrusion into my working productivity, then my frustration grows rapidly. My respect for that employee deteriorates at an alarming speed. Keep in mind that when circumstances of a highly productive associate require that they handle personal issues, there is seldom a problem. Their reputation has earned patience. Has yours?
>
> Your boss may or may not be singling out your behavior. Sure, you are upset, but ask yourself: What might have prompted the dramatic action of calling you on the carpet? Perhaps there have been numerous violations of work-personal abuse of time. As has been the case with the introduction of "casual days," some people exhibit good taste and others

do not. You know there exist misguided and often tasteless individuals who use the "freedom of choice" to dress inappropriately or worse.

Judgment, on the part of some employees, has been so poor in many companies that external consultants were hired to teach people how to dress properly. My only response to this expensive baby-sitting is: "Such measures confirm that too large of a segment of our society must be S.O.S. (Stuck On Shortsighted)." So, without greater knowledge of your situation, it is impossible to speak with insight. However, you probably know the level of abuse of company time by others in your organization.

There was a time when individuals were very sensitive about taking time during the workday for personal priorities. Also, in days gone by, there was an understanding that the time would be made up. Similarly, "way back in the 70's and 80's" the owners and operators of the business gave back time to employees when extra hours were required. After a couple of longish days, folks were invited to take a half-day for themselves. It was a two-way street of give and take and share and help. Such actions built trust and increased productivity.

Let me share one final thought regarding your concerns about your rights to privacy and e-mail. To obtain clarification about what is legal and appropriate, whether about your purchase of items for personal use on company time, or having the company monitor your e-mail, human resource professionals and legal counsel should be able to bring light to privacy and First Amendment rights. You should be aware, however, that any e-mail you send exists not only on your computer, but also on the company's server. It is more like a letter sitting open on someone's desk, than a sealed, first-class letter.

In the meantime, remember that integrity is congruence between what you say and what you do, as well as what you say about what you did.

Character issues are also involved when an employee learns of misconduct by the employer or an executive and decides whether or not to report the conduct to the appropriate authority. This "whistleblower" issue has always been troublesome, as Coleen Rowley of the Federal Bureau of Investigation (FBI) and Sherron Watkins of Enron can attest. Ms. Rowley became something of a celebrity for her castigation of the Minneapolis and national FBI culture as it impacted Minnesota FBI agents in their investigation of potential terrorists, including suspect Zacarias Moussaoui, even before the so-called "9-11 investigation," and whose efforts may have surfaced the attack plan before it occurred! Ms. Watkins told her

CEO in writing that something was amiss at Enron prior to that debacle. This issue of "whistleblowing" was presented by a reader who was faced with a similar, though less dramatic, situation.

Dear Jim:

Our company has an ethics hotline that is operated by an independent third party and all "tips" are treated anonymously. I have personal knowledge of a senior manager in the company who is taking sizeable gifts from groups to whom he awards work. There is no question in my mind that his actions are unethical. My question: Am I creating an ethical dilemma by not reporting this individual? I really don't want to do this but feel I have an obligation to do so. Please comment.

Response:

Assuming you trust the confidentiality of your corporation's hotline and assuming that you feel such violations of integrity could or will risk the future of your organization, then what choices are left to you?

1. Report unethical actions and affirm your values
2. Risk repercussions while strengthening your company values
3. Fulfill your obligations and exhibit social/corporate responsibility

If you cannot act, then you are becoming a participant in the ripping of the fabric of integrity that is the foundation of free enterprise.

If there are repercussions, then you have been lied to on the confidentiality issue. Would you then even want to work there?

The risks are real:

1. Remain in an ugly environment and build resentment
2. Respond and live with the consequences

To remain in an ugly environment carries risks that were brought home dramatically following World War II, in the War Crimes Tribunals held in Nuremburg, Germany. During those trials, many of the guards from the German prison camps claimed that they were innocent in the mass murder of their Jewish prisoners because they were only following orders. Recent cases in the media have shown that the "Nuremberg Defense" does not work, and therefore the employee faced with such an employer is truly "between a rock and a hard place." The practice of illegal instructions, however, continues, as can be seen in the following letter.

Dear Jim:

My boss has heard rumors that a former colleague of mine, who was fired, is thinking of suing our company. He has asked me to purge the files of anything that might be embarrassing or a problem for our firm if that lawsuit should be filed, before anything happens. Apart from the legalities that might be involved, I think this is unethical, and I am in a quandary about doing what I'm told in this case. What is your advice?

Response:

Get out of that moral cesspool as soon as possible. Everyone knows this type of behavior is not tolerated.

No integrity-centered organization would allow its supervisors, at any level, to place an employee in a compromising position such as the one you are describing. You are in a no-win situation. If you shred documents that you know could be important in a lawsuit, you could risk personal legal action. At that moment, at risk is not only your integrity, but also your vulnerability with our justice system.

On the other hand, if you do not follow the directives of your boss, you face charges of insubordination and could lose your job.

You need to address this problem head-on:

1. Are you sure you clearly understood the shredding directive?

2. If you did understand the shredding order, are you willing to face possible criminal charges for destroying evidence?

3. If you are not prepared to compromise your ethics or your reputation, then are you prepared to live without a paycheck should you be terminated for not carrying out an assignment?

4. Are there individuals in your current company to whom you can turn and blow the whistle on the person who has placed you in this quandary?

5. Would you feel comfortable going to your boss who suggested the shredding activity and asking whether the instructions to shred documents might be reconsidered? There are few people today who are not aware the risks and consequences of improper business behavior.

Begin planning immediately on ways that ensure that you will be spending the rest of your career in organizations whose ethics and integrity warrant your loyalty.

The character of companies viewed as a whole can present an opportunity for a useful discussion of integrity issues. Should a company be involved in the growing, production or sale of products known to bring harm to customers? If not, what of the whole economy related to those industries and what of the jobs that would go away? It is not our intention to pass judgment on those who do engage in these industries, so long as they are forthcoming about the risks and implications of their products and they do not engage in subliminal efforts to seduce people into the use of such products. Clearly, however, the boards of directors of such companies need to be extraordinarily vigilant. The obvious integrity issues related to the products of a company are not as dangerous as the subtle forms that creep into our society, described in the following letter.

Dear Jim:

Bob Herbert, a writer for *The New York Times*, states that our "nation is awash in credit debt" and he describes a family trapped in the vicious cycle of escalating costs. He tells the story of Julie and Jerry Pickett of Middletown, Ohio, who are still paying for groceries bought for their family years ago. They are trapped in the iron grasp of credit card debt, and he describes their situation as similar to problems faced in earlier days in this country when poorer people were loan-sharking victims. Are these credit card companies operating with integrity?

Response:

Unfortunately, the financial institutions which prey upon the poor would appear to be breaking no laws. Are they operating with integrity? Further analysis of the situation you describe could shed light on the some of the issues.

First, thank you for prompting me to read Mr. Bob Herbert's September 24, 2003, column. What he described was and is disturbing. After reading his thoughts, there are social issues raised that must not be swept under the rug in the name of making a buck. He tells us that people used to be jailed for what credit card companies now do legally. While banks and money markets are currently paying little interest to consumers, it is common for the effective annual percentage rate for balances on a friendly credit card to approach 30 percent. In the past this was an illegal practice called "usury."

Mr. Herbert's statistics present a grim reality for many in our society. Between 1989 and 2001, "credit card debt nearly tripled from $238 billion to $692 billion as many people resort to using credit cards to fight the ravages of unemployment and avoid disaster, while others battle the gap between declining real wages and rising home and essential health care costs. The savings rate steadily declined; bankruptcies jumped 125 percent, and the credit card debt of the average family increased by 53 percent. For middle class families, the increase was 75 percent. For senior citizens, it was 149 percent; and, families with annual incomes below $10,000 increased a staggering 184 percent.

According to Mr. Herbert, credit card companies have leapt gleefully into an orgy of exploitation, with late fees the fastest growing source of revenue for the industry. This fee category jumped from $1.7 billion in 1996 to $7.3 billion in 2002. Late fees now average $29, and most cards have reduced the late payment grace period from 14 days to 0 days. In addition to charging late fees, the major credit card companies use the first late payment as an excuse to cancel low introductory rates, often making a 0 percent card jump to between 22 and 29 percent. One ought not to assume that all credit card institutions behave this way. The information reported does suggest that increased monitoring might be constructive.

Since high rates are now legal, we must appeal to some sense of fair play, of ethical and moral behavior. Right thinking cannot accept this endless and costly treadmill for the less fortunate. It is not an appropriate dilemma for the poor, the less educated or the elderly. Something is "out of whack" when shrewd and financially gifted business decision-makers take advantage of the misery and misfortune of others. If such cruel and heartless business practices continue, free markets will suffer. Trust will deteriorate even further. The hope for living the American Dream might seem further away, and the children of our grandchildren might only read in history books what could have been their birthright: freedom and free markets! Simply because high rates are legal does not make them right. Integrity suggests that credit card institutions could lead the way in offering constructive solutions for these borrowers before it is too late. Here is an illustration where there is a real need to balance self-interest with social responsibility.

Without a motivated middle class there is no stability for this or any society. When the erosion of confidence outpaces the reward systems in place, chaos might become a way of life. Without mutual trust throughout our social and economic system, productivity declines along with confidence and motivation. Regulations can never replace relationships. However, when forced into a survival mode by greedy lenders, lawmakers will be forced to further regulate behaviors. There is still time to make things right and those who operate with and demand integrity-centered leadership behavior will need to lead the way. If those who prey upon the less fortunate do not change their ways, our society will wake up and demand even more stifling regulations, adding bureaucracy, with other, unanticipated, consequences. Unless behavior changes, regulation may be the only way out of the current abusive mess. Free markets must regulate themselves, or governments will. *Integrity* is what *matters*.

Where high interest rates are being charged, it is because skillful advisors are able to formulate the costs in the fine print of well-constructed legal agreements and sales contracts. In most cases, it is the character of the company involved in the activity that is pivotal, not the product or service itself. If the character of the company includes strong values that encourage honesty and openness, then the public will almost certainly be able to make fully informed decisions. If not, then the fine print can be expected to lead to the victimization of the customer. The character of an organization is the result of how its leadership behaves. Over time, the public will form a strong opinion of that character. A company's reputation is the sum total of the actions of the individuals who make up its leadership. The behavior of individuals in senior leadership positions of an organization build the reputation of their company one decision and action at a time, and the cumulative total can tell quite a story. Imagine if this decision process, described in the following letter, is repeated multiple times.

Dear Jim:

A friend in Hawaii has announced his retirement at age 55 from his employer of 21 years. He is in sales and recently told me that his boss put him on written warning for his performance last year, even though he met his sales quota. It was because he did not sell enough to one of the accounts per sales plan. My friend is 55 and cannot really afford to retire, but felt he was going to get forced out in a "youth movement" and did not want his work record to have on it the word "fired"!

I do not know all the facts; however, it does seem to me that when an employee has 20-plus years with a firm, having always been loyal to the organization, he deserves more than routine consideration. The behavior of the boss seems to lack integrity. It appears that this situation smells of constructive or wrongful discharge. What do you think?

Response:

Companies have the right to manage their operations in a variety of ways. They can legally hire and fire employees. Your friend is no exception. With reference to the integrity issue, we may find answers by first breaking down the concerns expressed in your letter.

Your friend announced his retirement, and for whatever reasons he chose this language, it may be difficult to undo this potentially legally binding announcement.

A written warning is a serious matter and may be associated with breaches of conduct that can outweigh other valuable contributions. For an outsider to comment on such actions by management might assume legal knowledge (even labor precedents) that rest beyond the practice of addressing integrity in leadership.

A career of 20 years, assuming competence, would certainly warrant due process. Your friend should have been keeping copies of every relevant document. If he has not done so, he should make every effort to secure them. Given the facts presented, it appears this person would be well-advised to follow a four-step process:

- Review his situation with the appropriate personnel professional.

- If things cannot be resolved satisfactorily, he should outline his alternatives and confirm them with his attorney.

- Seek a solution that does not "burn the bridge" for any future career opportunity with the company.

- Accept the reality that a solution that is not integrity-centered could force a separation that has legal, financial and emotional complications.

Legally, he may have boxed himself in. On the other hand, integrity-centered leadership could open a door for a more humane solution.

The decisions made by individuals in a leadership capacity are a product of their character. On April 17, 1997, President and Mrs. Clinton hosted "The

White House Conference on Early Childhood Development and Learning." We discovered that some expert psychologists believe that the character of an individual is largely formed by the time the person is about 10 years of age, while others put the character formation even earlier, by age 3. While subject to later influence, there is an essential character that each person has, that others come to view as that individual's reputation. This raises a question. Since none of us is perfect, are the flaws of each person cast in stone after our character is formed? Let us hope that there is always room for continuous improvement. One of our readers asked a character question enabling us to provide insight through two related stories.

Dear Jim:

How does one teach integrity to children? How does one pass along values? Are there any examples you might share?

Response:

The best teaching is by example. Our words are never as powerful as our actions. What we say is important. What we do makes all the difference. Rather than belabor the answer to your questions, please read the following two stories that were recently passed along to me from a reader of the "Integrity Matters" column and you will have the answers you are seeking.

(Story #1)

Many years ago, Al Capone virtually owned Chicago. Capone wasn't famous for anything heroic. His exploits were anything but praiseworthy. He was, however, notorious for enmeshing the Windy City in everything from bootlegged booze and prostitution to murder. Capone had a lawyer in Chicago nicknamed "Easy Eddie." He was his lawyer for a good reason. Eddie was very good! In fact, Eddie's skill at legal maneuvering kept Big Al out of jail for a long time. To show his appreciation, Capone paid him very well. Not only was the money big, but Eddie got special dividends. For instance, he and his family occupied a fenced-in mansion with live-in help and all of the conveniences of the day. The estate was so large that it filled an entire Chicago city block. Yes, Eddie lived the high life of the Chicago mob and gave little consideration to the atrocity that went on around him. Eddie did have one soft spot, however. He had a son that he loved dearly. Eddie saw to it that his young son had the best of everything: clothes, cars and a good education. Nothing was withheld. Price was no object. And, despite his involvement with organized crime, Eddie even tried to teach him right from wrong. Yes, Eddie tried to teach his son to rise above his own sordid life. Eddie wanted his son to be a better man than he was. Yet, with all his wealth and influence, there were two things he couldn't give his son, two things that Eddie sacrificed to the Capone mob that he couldn't pass on to his beloved son: a good name and a good example. One day, Easy Eddie reached a difficult decision. Offering his son a good name was far more important than all the riches he could lavish on him. Easy Eddie wanted to rectify all the wrong he had done. He decided he would go to the authorities and tell the truth about Al "Scarface" Capone; he would try to clean up his tarnished name and offer his son some semblance of integrity. But to do this, he would have to testify against The Mob, and he knew that the cost would be great. But more than anything, he wanted to be an example to his son. He wanted to do his best to make restoration and, hopefully, have a good name to leave his son. So, he testified. Within the year, Easy Eddie's life ended in a blaze of gunfire on a lonely Chicago street. But in his eyes, he had given his son the greatest gift he had to offer, at the greatest price he would ever pay.

(Story #2)

World War II produced many heroes. One such man was Lieutenant Commander Butch O'Hare. He was a fighter pilot assigned to the aircraft carrier Lexington in the South Pacific. One day his entire squadron was sent on a mission. After he was airborne, he looked at his fuel gauge and realized that someone had forgotten to top off his fuel tank. He would not have enough fuel to complete his mission and get back to his ship. His flight leader told him to return to the carrier. Reluctantly, he dropped out of formation and headed back to the fleet. As he was returning to the mother ship he saw something that turned his blood cold. A squadron of Japanese aircraft was speeding its way toward the American fleet. The American fighters were gone on a sortie, and the fleet was all but defenseless. He couldn't reach his squadron and bring them back in time to save the fleet. Nor could he warn the fleet of the approaching danger. There was only one thing to do. He must somehow divert them from the fleet. Laying aside all thoughts of personal safety, he dove into the formation of Japanese planes. Wing-mounted 50 calibers blazed as he charged in, attacking one surprised enemy plane and then another. Butch wove in and out of the now-broken formation and fired at as many planes as possible until all his ammunition was finally spent. Undaunted, he continued the assault. He dove at the planes, trying to clip a wing or tail in hopes of damaging as many enemy planes as possible and rendering them unfit to fly. He was desperate to do anything he could to keep them from reaching the American ships. Finally, the exasperated Japanese squadron took off in another direction. Deeply relieved, Butch O'Hare and his tattered fighter limped back to the carrier. Upon arrival he reported in and related the event surrounding his return. The film from the gun-camera mounted on his plane told the tale. It showed the extent of Butch's daring attempt to protect his fleet. He had in fact destroyed five enemy aircraft. This took place on February 20, 1942, and for that action Butch became the Navy's first Ace of World War II and the first Naval Aviator to win the Congressional Medal of Honor. A year later Butch was killed in aerial combat at the age of 29. His hometown would not allow the memory of this World War II hero to fade, and today, O'Hare Airport in Chicago is named in tribute to the courage of this great man. So the next time you find yourself at O'Hare International, give some thought to visiting Butch's memorial displaying his statue and his Medal of Honor. It's located between Terminals 1 and 2.

So what do these stories have to do with one another?

Butch O'Hare was Easy Eddie's son.

A mentor told me that "we teach best what we most need to learn," and perhaps that is why some of our greatest opportunities occur in moments of vulnerability. A poor role model, initially set by Butch O'Hare's father, became a source of greatness created through a father's courage. *Integrity matters.*

As outsiders, we can never know for sure what is in the mind and heart of a father and son, rather only what they say and do, as well as how they do it. Nevertheless, these two stories relating to Butch O'Hare do serve as a useful reminder of what is possible by the sheer power of personal conviction. Two more stories from our own experiences can help clarify this point.

(Story #1):

A senior male executive had scheduled a dinner for a group of 20 people at a conference. When he arrived at the appointed hour, many of the attendees had also arrived and were waiting. The maitre d' professed to have no reservation, clearly the person the executive had discussed this with on the telephone had neglected to write it down. The executive lost his cool. "Do you know who I am?" he demanded in a loud voice. "This is inexcusable, I'll have your job!" he went on, with more of the same. The manager came over, and assured the group there would be no problem, that they just needed a few minutes to put a table together for so large a group. The executive's demeanor did not soften. He told the manager, "You're darned right you will!" Members of his group were embarrassed by his display of emotion, and likely some clear and negative opinions about his leadership and values were formed that evening. One of his subordinates was heard to say to his wife, "You see what I'm faced with?" This executive might have normally behaved better; but who among his group would have known from the behavior he displayed?

(Story #2):

A different senior-level male executive was confronted with a similar situation, as it happens, but this time in Korea. He was preparing to enjoy a pre-dinner cocktail with some associates in the elegant lobby lounge of a five-star hotel in Seoul, Republic of South Korea. The order had been placed. Approaching the group, the normally poised waitress, beautifully coiffed and dressed in a pale green traditional silk "hanbok" (the Korean formal dress), stumbled on the carpeting, and the entire tray of drinks flew forward, in what was described as slow motion. The executive said that he watched the drinks become airborne, spin slowly through the air and land squarely in his lap, soaking his jacket, tie, shirt and pants. The waitress collapsed to her knees, and held her face. For a moment, the scene was frozen, but for her weeping apology.

The lounge manager arrived, bowed his profuse, formal apology to the executive and his companions, and made arrangements for the executive to occupy a room to change. Then in his native Korean Hangul language, sternly directed the waitress to follow, take the clothing, and have her personally clean it and dry it at once. This was done, and the waitress returned the clothing, neatly pressed, to the room within the hour.

In her Confucian culture, this waitress had shamed herself, her hotel and her family. There is not a concept of an accident in the Korean culture, and therefore she was viewed as guilty of a major personal transgression. Her job, her self-image and her self-worth were at risk.

The group that was convened by the executive, of course, waited with "drinks on the house" while the clothing was being cleaned. Upon returning to the lounge, and before rejoining the group, the executive made the effort to find the waitress and the manager and explained that he was impressed by the experience, and forgave the error of it. He suggested that the additional quiet time enabled him to reach some important decisions related to the business dealings that were the subject of the evening. Further, he told the manager that he considered this incident to be a sign of good fortune, and that he looked forward to being served by her on his future visits to the hotel.

No doubt his sensitivity helped her, and may well have saved her job. Moreover, his actions demonstrate how an executive can teach by example the true character of leadership.

The contrast in these two most recent stories is clear. When you find an individual like the one described in the second anecdote, appreciate, thank and treasure them. How we treat the people who serve us is one clear indication of character. It is by the example of men and women who behave in the manner of that visiting executive in Korea that confidence and trust in social norms are restored.

Character, after being restored, can be sustained when caring individuals "stand up" for what they believe in. This point is addressed in a letter from one of our readers.

Dear Jim:

I have read with interest your opinion on what eight "integrity-centered" questions to ask business leaders to determine the integrity level of their companies. My assumption is that our current business culture is simply a reflection of society in general and of the times in which we live. So, how can we hope to achieve an improvement in business ethics unless integrity starts guiding the actions of our political, educational and spiritual leaders? I am discouraged by the seemingly endless string of news stories highlighting greed and corruption among leaders in all areas. Is there anything we can do to make a difference?

Response:

Yes, you can make a difference. Individuals can have an impact. However, there are individual actions required in order to create changes in our cultural climate. First, you may want to answer these questions. The assumption made is that you can address each of these areas of concern with a gracious response, even though the position you choose to take may be quite strong.

1. When did you last write to your Congressional Representative expressing your concerns?

2. What is your response to sloppy service or behavior in a restaurant? A hotel? On public transportation? From a professional educator? A religious leader? Celebrities? Do you suffer in silence or communicate disappointment appropriately?

3. Do you practice courtesy even when confronted with rudeness?

4. Will you walk out of a movie theater or any performance when offended by the content or behavior?

5. Do you refuse to purchase, where practical, goods and services that sponsor programs and activities that conflict with your values? Including television programming?

6. Is what you profess to believe and value consistent with how you and your close friends behave?

7. Do those who know you best understand and respect your priorities?

8. Do you exhibit understanding and respect for the priorities of those you know best?

Second, assuming that you have addressed the eight questions above, you are now in a position to cause change. As a former President of the United States told a few of us, just about twelve years ago, "All politics is local." Change begins when each of us picks up the mirror and studies the reflection.

When you choose to take your "stand" generally determines the outcome.

People have not changed a great deal since the very beginning of time, all the way back to Adam and Eve and Cain and Abel. Human beings still make mistakes. A significant number of people are pretty good and others are rotten (at least from our perspective). Find the good ones and accept responsibility for change. In the last analysis, these ten two-letter words summarize what reality is; namely, to accept the responsibility that: "If it is to be, it is up to me." Because if it is true that integrity matters, then we must start with ourselves and those with whom we already have relationships. Beyond that, we are pretty much "at risk" unless we are willing to stand up, with those of like minds, to be counted.

Complain and do nothing and you can expect to be ignored, with continued misery.

Perceive wrong-headedness and act appropriately, and you will create a legacy of integrity.

To restore trust in our society will require that each of us works to strengthen our own character, and that of our leaders, with each action, and every day.

Chapter 5
HONESTY:
Truthful Communication

Where is there dignity unless there is honesty?
— Cicero (106 BC–43 BC)

Golf is a sport with a heritage of honesty. Even though some people do cheat at the game, the culture of golf has developed a certain respect for honesty. It is perhaps the only sport in which players routinely report penalties on themselves. Grantland Rice, the legendary sportswriter, said "Eighteen holes of match or medal play (golf) will teach you more about your foe than will 18 years of dealing with him across a desk."

Surely honesty would seem to be a simple concept: Honesty is the state of being truthful. An honest person is truthful consistently and without fail. An honest person does not permit fear, or personal inconvenience, to interfere with the truth. Such a person is truthful out of self-respect, and personal standards of conduct. Yet, an honest person may also have sensitivity, tact and compassion, and in such a combination may engage in balancing truth with timing and propriety. The following example illustrates this issue.

A man was sitting at the hospital bedside of his close friend, who was dying of cancer, and whose son had recently been arrested in another city for selling drugs. The dying man, unaware of the arrest, asked the man, "Where is my son? Surely he will come to see me before I die?"

The man, knowing his friend would probably die within the hour, simply replied, "He is making every effort to get here quickly, but most flights are booked."

This man, who was careful in what he said to his dying friend, would certainly not lose his reputation for honesty because of this kindness. Honesty is about how we treat others in terms of forthrightness and fairness. There are occasions when despite our best efforts, we miss the mark in getting our ideas across. A favorite quote, whose source is lost to us, is "I know you think you understand what you thought I said, but I'm not sure you understand that what you thought I said is not what I meant!"

Any husband who has been asked by his wife, "Honey, how do I look?" as she dressed for an important evening, or any wife who has asked her husband, "How much did you spend?" on anything from the golf clubs to the flowers he brought home for her, knows that honesty can have some complexity. Further, we know that honesty is more than simply words. Body language, from the shake of a head to the folding of arms, can communicate a response. Certainly silence conveys meaning, and therefore contributes to the communication of honesty. For example, if an executive is asked for a reference on a former employee, the response of silence is a profound communication. Silence communicates, yet the meaning is under the control of the receiver. In fact, if we return to the first example in this paragraph, regarding the wife's question about her appearance, the response of silence might be the most risky communication of all!

Smooth-talking politicians have long been masters of positioning their words so that they can shift the meaning of their statements as a matter of convenience. We all know of people who will deny their statements when quoted later, as "I never said that!" or "That's not what I said." or "You've taken my remarks out of context." Many of us were alive to watch President Nixon deny knowledge of the Watergate break-in. And we were later saddened to hear on the tape recordings from the Oval Office that he did have knowledge of the events surrounding Watergate. He had lied to the people. More recently, we were disappointed again as we watched President Clinton state, "I did not have sex with that woman!" and then quibble over the meaning of the word "is." Yet in a later plea bargain, he admitted to the charge of obstruction of justice.

Other forms of dishonesty are less direct. When an accountant knowingly classifies an expense item as a capital cost, so that it can be depreciated over time rather than charged against current income, that person is not being honest. There have been many examples in recent years of accountants engaging in this sort of dishonesty, involving companies such as Enron, WorldCom and Tyco. When an individual paints an automobile to hide the rust in anticipation of a higher sales price, dishonesty has occurred. Honesty has taken a beating, as well, when a news network chooses to highlight a bonfire in such a way as to suggest wholesale rioting is taking place in order to embellish the news. It is not appropriate to wink when fraud occurs. Lying and cheating are wrong.

Honesty is more than simple truthfulness. Honesty derives from respect for others, as well as one's self, and that includes tactful respect for the feelings of other people. Over time, organizations take on the culture presented by their leaders.

When the leaders value honesty, it becomes a part of the culture of their organization. One of the readers of "Integrity Matters" asked a question along these lines.

Dear Jim:

What obligation for truthfulness does management have with employees? Obviously, Enron stepped over the line by outright lying to employees. But how much truth is enough? When business prospects are down, when consolidations or reorganizations are being considered, when units are being sold or spun off, when business strategies change—all with potentially adverse impact on employees' continued employment—how much information should be shared with those being impacted?

Response:

Management has 100 percent responsibility to deal with all of its stakeholders truthfully. Leaders provide appropriate information ... as they see it. Sometimes optimism may seem naïve in hard times. When circumstances fail to improve, then these same leaders can be accused of ignorance or malfeasance. They make mistakes.

However, leadership can never skirt the truth. Timing of the telling of the truth requires judgment, which can be imperfect.

Great leaders err on the side of disclosure. Look for patterns and act accordingly. If someone lies one time, that is an event, or, perhaps, even a misunderstanding. If they lie twice, there is a pattern. If they lie a third time, it has become a habit. Habits are hard to change.

Earlier, we spoke of accountants misclassifying expenses, as a way of misrepresenting the truth. This practice can have significant public impact, as the following reader describes.

Dear Jim:

I lost money in the stock market, because some company executives were using very questionable accounting practices. The audit committees of these companies either didn't care or were ignorant about what was going on. What can be done to bring some integrity into the business world?

Response:

First, acknowledge that a lot of integrity already exists in the "business world"! An overwhelming number of times each day, all over the world, including in the United States, people "Say what they do and do what they say." Milk from the carton is pure. Trash is removed. Police protect us. Goods and services are traded fairly and professionally. All in all, we have a solid foundation for commerce.

The problem is greed. Fool me once, shame on you. Fool me twice, shame on me. When we refuse to do business with self-serving, greedy, unreliable business people, the market itself will run them off.

Governmental laws will never take the place of individuals confronting "colleagues" with honest rebuke. We need to see the pendulum swing toward responsiveness and responsible business practices. The pendulum will be moved when it is nudged by our elected officials, the media and appropriately principled leaders (in all walks of life). Those are the leaders who are willing to stand up and be counted.

Make a personal effort to compliment those who impress you with integrity and to criticize (professionally) those who violate the principle. One at a time, we become the people we need to be.

The idea that we need to see the pendulum swing toward more professional integrity is also true of the media, which enjoy a special trust with the public to represent the truth of events in our communities and around the world. Recent incidents have taught us that it is wrong to protect someone who does not possess that degree of professional integrity out of a misguided sense of mentorship, as the following exchange demonstrates.

Dear Jim:

The New York Times has just apologized for the fraudulent work of one of its reporters. That is all well and good. But *The Times* enjoys a public trust, and surely they have a responsibility to spot check or verify the work of their featured writers to ensure that such a fiasco is never allowed to happen. At the end of the day, it seems that you cannot trust what you see on television, or what you read in newspapers. What do you think?

Response:

Please do not overreact to the dishonesty of a writer for *The New York Times*. There are rotten apples everywhere, and this fraud was caught. Further, in what turns out to be thorough follow-up, the very same newspaper confronted its errors and exposed its own vulnerabilities for what they were and are: human. Con artists come in lots of forms, including writers.

Several years ago, Johnson & Johnson, the makers of Tylenol, acknowledged that a few of their packages had been compromised and that rather than risk any further harm to the public, that every Tylenol product would be removed from the shelves, everywhere and immediately. They had taken responsibility for the crisis and avoided permanent disaster. Today, in part because of the Tylenol crisis, Johnson & Johnson has enhanced it stellar position in the world of business and integrity.

The Times may have set a similar standard of honesty and integrity with its ownership and accountability of its own blunders: publishing materials that had not been verified and hiring and retaining a dishonest and unprofessional news writer. To be sure, their own follow-up investigation and subsequent reporting of the story was hard hitting and offered no excuses. ... Upon careful reading of our definition and assuming *The Times* management team continues to follow through, they will be able to stand tall in the arena of responsible and responsive leadership. Integrity is congruence between what you say and what you do, as well as what you say about what you did. Integrity is the keystone of leadership. The keystone holds the enterprise together at its most critical junction, where ideas, products and services meet the customer. The keystone enables the arch to fulfill its supportive mission. Integrity enables an organization to achieve its mission. Integrity is the strength, unity, clarity and purpose that upholds and sustains all of the activities of the enterprise. Integrity provides this stabilizing dimension by never, ever, compromising. Integrity recognizes risks and assumes responsibility. It drives the realization of vision toward the enterprise's destination. Leaders exude integrity.

Based upon what *The Times* has done to rectify its mistakes, which is to maintain your confidence (and our confidence) in our freedom of the press, then we should applaud their efforts to regulate themselves. Our system is not perfect, nor is our press; however, we can be reassured that integrity does matter, and especially with our media, as was demonstrated by their good-faith efforts to be upfront with their problems and their immediate steps to address issues.

Based upon the definition of integrity provided by the Bracher Center for Integrity in Leadership, *The New York Times* has thus far lived up to every promise in this.

Not only companies misrepresent the truth, of course. We see many examples of individuals changing the facts to obtain a larger insurance settlement, or misrepresenting a situation for their economic advantage. Honesty can be the victim of misrepresentation, as well as outright falsehood. Because honesty is normally assumed in our interpersonal dealings, the opportunity to misrepresent motives exists. Furthermore, the natural tendency to assume straightforward relationships can leave a business open to possible victimization. The following letter presents a relevant question about the honesty of certain career-oriented individuals:

Dear Jim:

My insurance company hires aspiring younger people, those between ages 28 and 40, then we spend about two years educating and training them in our specialty. We open our client files to these newcomers to our industry and we equip them for success using our knowledge and experience. We pay them while they learn and expect them to re-pay us with several years of service and loyalty.

Over the past decade, and especially more recently, we have noticed a very disappointing trend. These valuable individuals leave us shortly after their two-year orientation and take with them our contacts and our intellectual property, seemingly without remorse or guilt. When confronted, their responses vary, but one theme bursts through all of their explanations and rationalizations: We are doing nothing that is illegal.

Is this an integrity issue? If it is, how can we address it and stop this waste of time and money?

Response:

Integrity is at the heart of your story, really saga, of individuals landing on board your insurance boat, eating your business food, only to leave your employment with the mess created by their premature exit. Their respect for your investment in them (these individuals) is absent. There appears to be an abdication, on their part, of any responsibility for returning some portion of the training costs. When these trainees mention that what they are doing is not illegal, they seem to be saying that relationships and accountability are not the cornerstones of the social contract they are honoring.

How sad for you and how very tragic for these individuals and the values they are using to build the future.

The tone of your question communicates that you understand the importance of character in the transaction of business. The following definition might easily describe how you operate.

Character:

Character is the ability to carry out the resolution long after the initial burst of enthusiasm is gone. Character shows when decisions are implemented. Character is the sum total of behaviors and is most completely demonstrated when individuals perform under pressure. Graciousness is almost always part of effective leadership character. Leaders with character drive organizational culture in all actions.

Loyalty is a two-way street that has been clogged with selfishness and self-serving leaders across multiple industries. You are reaping the whirlwind of brutal layoffs and shortsighted strategies that have been highlighted by the media for a quarter of a century. It has now become a game of who can take theirs first. For those who play this game, trust has moved to the back of the line.

Please do not give up on the next generation. From the letters received here, through the "Integrity Matters" column, the search is still on for high-quality firms. There are individuals, many of them, who are looking for integrity-centered leadership. Their desire is to find a worthy mission and work toward its accomplishment. They are not afraid to commit. They are eager to learn. They are willing to give back.

One of my favorite advisors, a retired founder of an insurance company that grew quite large, told me that his key to growing his successful organization centered in three questions he asked of himself after he interviewed prospective employees.

1. Did he like the person? Over a meal, it becomes fairly obvious if one enjoys being with the other person. If you really do not enjoy their company, why hire them?

2. Had the individual ever had to sacrifice? Had they overcome humble beginnings? Were they an accomplished musician, athlete, speaker, user of a second or third language? Did they work while attending college?

3. What was and is their divine factor? What did they do for others simply because they wanted to? Do they enthusiastically give to charities (whether in terms of money or time)?

When you can answer affirmatively to these three areas, there is an improved chance that the individual will see the partnership and obligation. Such individuals have integrity.

In the meantime, maintain your standards and hold your course. Good people are out there.

There are many fine people out there, and this is also true among employees in industries that have suffered considerable public embarrassment. The "dot-com collapse" in the stock market in the early days of the 21st century generated a number of honesty concerns regarding the investment community. An "Integrity Matters" reader raises a serious question arising out of significant financial (and hence, personal) setbacks:

Dear Jim:

Over the past several years, I have watched our economy sputter. Big dreams for early and comfortable retirement for my wife and me have evaporated. We are partly responsible for the difficulties. We, no, really I am mostly the one who pushed for higher returns on investments. We kept reading about these high technology projects that had tremendous valuations for their stocks. I insisted that we jump in and enjoy the returns. When things began to fall apart, the advice my wife and I received was to "stay the course, stocks are a long-term investment." We trusted our investment advisors.

We lost about 60 percent of our funds.

Was our tremendous loss related to the integrity of those who sold the investments and counseled us? Was this an integrity issue for those who were the leaders of the companies in which we invested? I am willing to accept responsibility for every dollar lost, primarily because I must. Yet, there were people (advisors, venture capitalists, corporate executives and investment bankers) who must have known more than we did. Many of them bought in early, watched the stock price catapult, then they bailed out and left us to go down with the sinking ship.

I am angry, embarrassed and a lot poorer. Whose integrity can one trust?

Please help, because I am in over my head or maybe simply a victim of fraud.

Response:

Your situation is all too common. You feel taken advantage of, and there are legitimate reasons for your feelings. You may or may not be a sophisticated investor. You may or may not have close friends who are wise in the ways of finance and investments. You may or may not have legal recourse, even though you may believe that those in control of your investments could have advised you to sell before risking so much of your money.

Here is the irony and the sad truth of a seemingly modern and wealthy society. Long ago, in the Middle Ages, many of the leaders of the Catholic Church kept language and education away from many deserving and capable people. Instead of educating the masses, the power hungry of this earlier time kept writing, reading, math and science in the hands of the few. In that medieval era, the few were primarily members of the "club" made up of church leaders (clerics and bishops). An exclusive club back then was wrong in the ways it treated those who trusted it, and it is wrong today.

As a consequence of the actions, freedom was kept in check and a certain theological aristocracy operated pretty much as it chose. That period of time was often called the Dark Ages, not simply because people were unable to educate themselves through reading and study, but also because the world was lit only by fire. The Middle Ages had only the intellectual light offered by those in power. Any other light was from the fires that warmed their humble homes, cooked their meals and tortured those who challenged accepted rules and regulations. A fascinating book addressing this medieval integrity crisis is *A World Lit Only by Fire: The Medieval Mind and the Renaissance Portrait of an Age*, by William Manchester.

The situation today is remarkably similar. Medieval priests reading and speaking Latin have been replaced in our era by balance sheet wizards and magicians of money. Instead of a Dark Ages being manipulated by well-read theologians with power and prestige, today we are surrounded by articulate and sophisticated gurus of finance, banking and capital formation.

They are well-trained in these modern times to speak in a language calculated to be beyond the "average" wage earner whose dollars have disappeared. It seems that many of "the best" of graduate business institutions pride themselves on the privileged alumni that they helped to educate. More recently this "elite society" has begun including women. These communities of privilege communicate an image ... that they own and can manipulate the financial transactions of our nation and a significant portion of the world. Unfortunately, in many instances, they do.

Financial power, consolidated in the hands of the few, no matter how well-educated, can too easily place personal greed and club-membership loyalty (to those already "in") far above integrity. Feelings of exclusivity abound and those outside the circle may not receive appropriate advice and counsel. In fact, your story is not unique.

Encouraging beginning or unsophisticated investors to participate in these inflated valuations, fabricated by members of the "financial wizards club" is wrong. Keeping them in these inflated transactions long after they should have exited is borderline corrupt. It may not be illegal, but most assuredly it is immoral. Too often the "off the street" investor was losing a small family fortune while those in the know, who invested early, were taking high profits and bailing out. These friends of the "magicians of money" knew the game and played it well. Those outside the club circle suffered reversals of fortunes that left them devastated in lots of ways.

If you do not understand the investment enterprise, are not 100 percent confident that your counselor really works for you, then you are playing in a game that offers a low risk of winning, or sometimes, even surviving.

What has been going on relative to the making of money is not right. Using insider information, parsing words and avoiding giving prudent counsel are some of the symptoms of an elite group run amok. Society will be healthy again when we reject the fraudulent behavior and reward integrity-centered advisors, just as the Reformation worked to cure the ills of the Middle Ages.

Obviously, there are honest professionals in finance and investments. It is important that you know a great deal about their skills, credentials and motivations. The very best way to learn about advisors (financial and others) is to review their track records with those who have worked with them before. History is often an excellent way to predict or at least better understand the future.

On a personal note, I am very sorry for what you and others suffered during these recent times, specifically as you sought ways to secure your retirement years.

What, then, about the honesty of businesses that exploit those who are not fortunate enough to have investment funds? The opportunities that exist to take advantage of the working poor are many, for among such people there generally exists less financial sophistication. An honest company will look out for people to make sure they understand what they are getting into; the dishonest company will look for opportunities to take advantage of people who are frightened by the actual or imagined complexities of financial matters, including taxes. In the following letter, a reader questions this type of practice.

Dear Jim:

I read in our paper that "Quick Tax Loans Cost Taxpayers almost $2 Billion." Further, these check-cashing fees add to the cost of getting tax refunds and loans. And the worst part is that these fees are targeted at the working poor. What kind of integrity is this? What is the thinking of those who prepare the taxes for the working poor as well as those who make available their financial institutions to assist in carrying out this high-cost activity? Is everything about money, no matter who is taken advantage of?

Response:

You have raised an issue that is central to the integrity of our society. We are supposed to protect those who cannot protect themselves. And, our society is judged by how we respond to those at high risk.

The working poor are an admirable segment of our society. At one time or another, most of us had immigrant ancestors who came to the United States of America as "the working poor" and found independence and success; economic and otherwise. Working poor means that these are individuals not asking for a "pass"—they have taken a job and they are contributing. They work in hopes of finding what Americans have always dreamed about, a better life through effort, sacrifice and commitment. Taking advantage of this group is awful.

Having done research about this tax-refund and loan process, where a number of tax preparation organizations, some being quite large, and certain financial institutions charge high fees and interest rates, it is difficult not to be appalled. Their leaders respond that if they did not supply these expensive services, then someone else would. Whether they are right or wrong, we should be thoughtful in hurrying to find a scapegoat. Blaming accountants and bankers is not productive. The solutions lie in the hands of those who regulate these types of actions, namely, our government officials.

Without an upward success path for the working poor in our society, they are left with little hope and motivation. If you feel, as I do, that this callous manipulation of our emerging workforce is wrong, then contact the Attorney General's office in your state. Unless free markets (in this case, the tax preparers and their collaborating financial institutions) are willing to regulate themselves, then governments will. If what is being done is legal, then find out how to change the laws. Right now, in these harsh times, we all need one another.

Preying on the working poor, reducing an already small amount of money that is rightfully theirs, by taking advantage of their lack of knowledge and sophistication, says a lot about the character and integrity of those who know the ropes and utilize the loopholes.

One loophole available to the dishonest person is the excuse that "I didn't know," or "I didn't realize," or even "I made a simple mistake." One of the more public questions of honesty in this category occurred in baseball. No one but Sammy Sosa, right fielder for the Chicago Cubs, knows the truth in this issue. His use of a corked bat attracted national media attention for weeks, and generated the following letter.

Dear Jim:

Yesterday, June 3, 2003, in a major league baseball game in Chicago, Illinois, with the Chicago Cubs playing against the Tampa Bay Devil Rays, superstar Sammy Sosa of the Cubs used an illegal corked bat, and the media are having a field day. Why are corked bats illegal? And, if they are illegal in regular competition, why do they exist at all? The alleged purpose is to use them in exhibitions; but does that not render exhibitions a fraud?

Finally, no matter what the explanation, since Sammy is a professional ball player, wouldn't he recognize immediately that the heft and feel of the bat were different? Therefore, I believe that he has broken a trust with the fans. Do you agree?

Response:

This is an embarrassing moment in the life of this columnist. For more years than I care to remember, the Summer Slump of the Cubs has rendered me helpless, distraught, sometimes speechless and often broken-hearted. They really know how to grind away at the self-confidence of young and old fans alike; and maybe that is what makes them the Cubs. Matters become even worse when the Chicago Cubs blunder in September. So, with that tidbit of bias on the table, let me respond.

First, it would be wonderful for baseball if Sammy Sosa could come forward and say: "It just ain't so!" (He would need to communicate that the incident was not of his making and the bat did not belong to him.) Second, let us then hope that the "corked bat incident" was truly a mistake and will never happen again.

In the meantime, let's live in the real world. This story is about market economics and individual greed. Your questions about "corked bats" are unsettling and your insights with reference to knowledge and accountability are powerful.

The lawyers and the media are likely to have a field day asking a few of their favorite questions:

1. What did he know?

2. When did he know it?

3. Can there be an explanation or a loophole that makes the whole thing go away?

4. What is the definition of 'cork'?

5. Who needs to take the blame for this so that nobody loses any money?

The fans have another set of questions:

1. Why would a superstar need to cheat?

2. Why would a high-potential future Hall-of-Famer ever risk his reputation by even possessing an illegal piece of equipment anywhere near the field of play?

3. Why would Sammy risk simply getting an illegal hit over his team's success?

4. Is major-league baseball so desperate for money from fans that it looks the other way when illegal bats are used during exhibitions (home run competitions)?

Back to your question about Sammy Sosa: Has he broken a trust? We do not know, yet. What we do know is that major league baseball officials are examining bats that they believe belonged to Sammy. Should there be any compromised bats, then the legal system that governs major league baseball will determine guilt.

The bigger issue is recognizing that what is natural (a baseball bat and a baseball, neither of which has been juiced up) seems no longer adequate for the entertainment expectations of certain fans, owners and players. Baseball appears to have turned toward the "carnival atmosphere" and risks making a farce of what once was referred to as "our National Pastime."

Legitimate games, at whatever level, from amateurs on the sandlot to the professionals in big league parks, are designed to place every participant on the same fair playing field. When greed displaces legitimate competition, then cheating creeps in, and integrity has become little more than a catch phrase punctuated by the wink of the carnival barker.

If this recent Sammy Sosa "corking the bat" incident is properly addressed, then baseball will be the stronger and fans will not lose confidence in the sport, its players, the owners or the agents. Do we really need a corked bat anywhere, anytime or for any reason? If not, get rid of them, once and for all.

Should all parties not be forthright, however, in communicating the circumstances that led to the event; and should appropriate evidence not be presented regarding the real problems (creating false images of players hitting baseballs incredible distances, with illegal bats)—then the ticket-purchasing public, the fans, will have reason to assume that fraud and deceit are alive and well—even with major league baseball. Confidence in the integrity of baseball will suffer yet another blow. Any actions short of full disclosure will simply create another corporate scandal covered over with "cork" and empty promises about truth, honest competition and integrity in leadership.

Oh, Sammy, say it isn't so!

Of course, Sammy did say, "It isn't so," that he "made a simple mistake," and only he knows for sure. Ultimately, he will be judged on his future behavior over the balance of his career. If, at the time of his retirement, Sammy Sosa has never again been held suspect, then history will perhaps come down on the side of believing his statements and judge in his favor. Time, as they say, will tell.

What we do know for sure is that most children experiment with honesty early in their formative years. When caught in an error, the child will try a statement something like, "I didn't do it," or "(Joe) did it!" Usually, the withering look of a mother is all that is necessary for the truth to come out, and most children learn over time that the truth is the better course. In this way, the important value of honesty is learned. Children who learn this later in life can change their behavior to include honesty as a preferred style. If the child's character has not been properly nurtured, the individual may lapse into dishonesty under pressure or stress.

Honesty becomes part of a organization's culture through the behavior of its leaders—not some of the time; not most of the time, but all of the time. Rebuilding corporate cultures, making integrity-centered leadership the keystone is the only path. Following the integrity-centered path requires the selection and development of leaders who place honesty as their highest value, as well as the removal of those who do not operate in the same way.

A retired judge once shared the following bit of wisdom with regard to the truth. He said that it is not only important to render the right decision, but also for it to be recognized as the right decision.

The restoration of trust cannot be built upon the bitter clay of dishonesty—it requires the fertile soil of truth.

Chapter 6
OPENNESS:
Operational Transparency

Clearly spoken, Mr. Fogg; you explain English by Greek.
– Benjamin Franklin

Around 1980, a contractor near Dallas, Texas, was building a number of new homes in a development. The model house was impressive, with brick external walls, wonderful landscaping and superb woodwork inside. However, the walls didn't quite seem square to those who were considering buying the house. Finally, when asked about this, the builder became excited and escorted the potential buyers to the kitchen. "You've got to see this," he said with pride. Once in the kitchen, he pointed out the mirror that was on an angled wall, facing the food-preparation island and cutting board at the kitchen's center. He pushed on the mirror, which turned out to be an entryway into a small room with a desk, chair and library. He proudly informed the prospective buyers that the mirror was one-way glass, and that an individual could sit in the library and watch the kitchen while hidden from view in this secret room. This, he said, explained the angles of the walls of the other rooms. His message? "Things are not always what they seem." The couple shopping for a home that day didn't buy the house or any other from this contractor because they questioned his integrity. If the contractor was so intrigued and delighted by a hidden room, they thought, what else might he be hiding?

In the preceding chapter, we were reminded of the importance of telling the truth if we value a reputation for integrity. There can be no place for falsehood, sneaky behavior, hidden agendas, manipulation or dishonesty masquerading as the truth. Yet, the dilemma exists: If we are to place trust in our institutions and in each other, then an open society, in which things are what they appear to be, is essential. The question becomes one of balance. A person of good character possesses that balance. A company that has achieved standing in the world as one of good character would have achieved that balance as well, and in the process could be expected to have lower turnover, greater customer loyalty and therefore higher profits over time.

The character of an organization is the sum of the character of its leadership. Every leader, or aspiring leader, must learn to deal with the requirement of being open and sometimes, being alone. It means that people will intrude upon one's perceived need for privacy, but openness requires a level of trust, of letting other people have the opportunity to see things as they are. When operational transparency is working, there is always the chance that some well-meaning "back seat driver" will want to influence the thinking of another person. Openness means caring, demonstrating concern and being willing to show vulnerability. Leaders make decisions alone. This requires self-acceptance, which is recognizing one's strengths, as well as vulnerabilities, and proceeding with the risk of exposing one's self to criticism.

A reader of "Integrity Matters" posed a question that illustrates the need for openness, specifically as it pertains to the Roman Catholic Church's recent struggles with improper clerical behavior.

> Dear Jim:
>
> The sexual abuse scandal in the Roman Catholic Church has not been handled well by those in charge. In your opinion, will that part of the Church suffer in membership growth in the years ahead? Will other faith-based groups or churches be tarnished by what has happened with the Romans? In other words, do people at large see a difference in religious groups or do they just lump them all together?

Response:

> Society is tarnished by abusive behaviors. Such behaviors corrupt and, when ignored, degenerate from corrosive to destructive. They cost any institution its reputation, productivity and support—financial and otherwise. It is bad business for the church. It is bad business for government. It is bad business, period.
>
> Human beings, however, do perceive differences, both subtle and obvious. At least one can assume such thoughtfulness of those who see wrong behavior, whether in business, politics or the church. When stresses increase and individuals feel fear, economic or cultural, there can be a tendency to "close ranks" and "harden" judgments.

At this time in history, integrity is under attack, whether by commission or omission, and levels of trust are eroding in too many areas.

Short-term: People may lump religious leadership into one category
or another.

Long-term: Society will "right" itself and balance will be restored.

Short-term: Those looking for reasons to discount spirituality along
with organized religion will find "reasons."

Long-term: Those predisposed to take spirituality seriously will continue to do so. Even imperfect religious organizations, founded to spread
the message of love, compassion, repentance and forgiveness, will experience certain renewal and restoration.

If leaders in government, business and education can change how
they function by becoming more responsive to their constituencies, then
religious leadership can as well.

Conclusion: Maintain the long view of history and have faith in the
common sense of most people. Legitimate values remain. Know your
own, seek those who share your priorities and be ready to "blow the
whistle" on those who attempt to corrupt that which you hold precious.
After all, integrity matters.

Organizations concerned with spirituality have periodically had their problems. However, as these organizations are focused upon values, they tend to root
out their hypocrisies and experience renewal once these errors do come to light
and, as a result, they have regained the trust of their constituents. The current
episode in the Roman Catholic Church is agonizing for those involved, and hun-
dreds, if not thousands, of media stories have focused on the issues of pedophilia and the subsequent cover-ups. This church will right itself, but secrecy has
been the fuel for the growth of the problem. Complaints were covered up. Offend-
ing priests were transferred to other parishes. Victims were sometimes blamed for
the problems. As the scandals unfolded, information was withheld from public
view and even in some cases, from the authorities attempting to investigate the
allegations. Not only were the crimes concealed and allowed to continue over the
years, they were even perpetuated as this church came to be seen as a haven for
these deviant personalities. This saga is a classic example of the need for the operational transparency that is essential to prevent those with darker motivations
from engaging in destructive behavior.

Obviously, other church organizations have also suffered scandals in past
years, and spiritual organizations are not the only types of institutions that engage

in cover-ups. Recent business scandals have shown that cover-ups also occur in the corporate world. The following letter, received in early 2003, describes one such problem.

Dear Jim:

How dare the executives of a major airline grant bonuses to themselves without disclosing same, at the very time they are asking their unions to make major financial concessions? Of course they can do it— it is not illegal—but where is the integrity here? Shame on them!

Response:

Your letter singles out airline executives as exhibiting conduct unbecoming leaders. You are right that they behaved poorly; however, they are not alone in the airline industry, nor are they unique in much of the current business environment. The executive "perk" is an innocent-sounding word that covers a multitude of greed-driven activities. A significant number of these "big shots" have been playing both sides of the fence in areas of salary, stock, free loans, gigantic bonuses, travel, disability insurance, health coverage and a list of self-serving services that cause many in their organizations to feel the top brass lives in the penthouse, while the majority of the workers feel relegated to the outhouse.

You might also be aware that another airline ... recently asked its pilots to accept reduced work schedules without pay to save money. Shortly after the pilots accepted what they believed was a good-faith proposal, headquarters declared multi-millions in special executive bonuses. A short while later, under significant pressure from their disgruntled employees, especially the pilots, those airline executives revisited their earlier bonus decisions and said they had behaved inappropriately. The truth is the executives blew it. This level of misbehavior reminds me of the insensitivities of the French nobility just before the Revolution of 1789. Widely attributed to Marie Antoinette (but more likely Jean-Jacques Rousseau), the story has followed through the years that, when the masses were starving, begging for the basics of life, bread, she is reported to have said, "Let them eat cake!"

It is now—and will remain—an issue of integrity. Productive citizens know that they must have an environment that creates trust, or the fabric of faith in the system is torn, sometimes beyond simple repair. These "unprofessional" behaviors are not exclusively about "perks" for those in the penthouse; they are about greedy and shortsighted power brokers abandoning social responsibility and accountability. Each of us, and most especially those in leadership roles, are responsible for leaving society stronger than we found it. Sacrifice, when not shared appropriately by all of the stakeholders, becomes unnecessary suffering for those further down the food chain.

We need our leaders to lead with integrity. Integrity is the keystone of leadership. It is reflected in discussions, decisions, directives and diagnostics. Integrity-centered leaders do not worry about taking care of themselves at the expense of those who work with and for them. Leadership emerges from listening, demonstrates character in behavior, and leverages energy with integrity. Sharing the good times and the tough times together is what builds confidence and trust throughout an organization. Integrity is the stabilizing factor that sustains effort and causes energy to create the canopy for accomplishment. Integrity enables the achievement of Vision. Integrity guides responsible decision-making and effective leadership.

Public companies face legal requirements for disclosure, but these regulations may fall short of what we mean by an "open culture." Often there is information that, if known, would alter employee perception of an organization, but which can legally be kept secret. For example, during the time when public attention was being given to South Africa as its citizens struggled to end apartheid, some companies were tempted to remain quiet about agency relationships with affiliates working in South Africa. Some companies even made efforts to appear not to be doing business in the country of South Africa when in fact they were! This is not unlike the shell game played by some individuals who hide their assets when confronted with a legal judgment. At some level it is the same as manipulating words to change the meaning of an event or a commitment.

There are other areas of society in which openness is at times difficult to discover, including that segment responsible for the education of future leaders. Openness is not only an issue in industry, it's an area of concern in the academic community as well, as can be seen in the following exchange with a reader. The letter speaks to the issue of shared credit (in this instance, compensation) for academic or consulting research (although this practice is apparently understood and accepted in certain academic settings).

Dear Jim:

A professor at our university is using his students to do research for which he is charging a company consulting fees. Shouldn't he either be paying the students or donating the work? Am I wrong to see this as unethical?

Response:

Yes, you may be wrong to see this behavior as unethical—without more information. Professors in some academic institutions are allowed, even encouraged, to conduct research and provide expertise. Depending upon the nature of this professor's contract with the academic institution and the client, there may be no conflict or interest.

Students provide lots of "low-cost" services to institutions of higher learning.

One clear example is major college football, which generates large amounts of cash through ticket sales. These athletic activities can provide generous compensation packages for certain instructors and coaches. Perhaps your question is addressing the legality of such activities.

In that area, please consult legal counsel.

If your concern is that students should be paid for learning techniques and processes that could later benefit their own careers (post education)—that could raise yet another question: Is the "work" of the students only "billable" because the professor supervises the interpretation? Is this a form of "sweat equity"?

In this instance, integrity and morality do not seem to be "on the block." Judgment may be. In the meantime, enjoy sports activities and special grants that enable institutions of higher education to improve salaries and benefits for those who choose to serve our future generations through academic service.

Our universities provide a rich resource of talent for our economy. Educational institutions have provided thousands of information technology graduates, who have, in turn, provided the capabilities for the rise of the Internet. These new companies created a marketplace through the World Wide Web. Some of the high-tech companies were prime movers in the computer and software industries and became closely associated with the rise of the "dot-com" companies during the late 1990's. The dot-com collapse (as well as the decline of the stock market) during the first years of the new century was not, however, caused by the academic community, but rather by greed. This economic debacle certainly raised a number of questions about openness, as some companies were formed using seductive promises with little substance. One of the more interesting questions addressed to "Integrity Matters" illustrates the disastrous economic impact on some investors that resulted from the shadowy investment practices of those "go-go" years.

Dear Jim:

In the past few days I have read that more rules may be needed to ensure companies put enough money into their pension funds for employees. Some corporations have made overly optimistic projections of their future earnings, allowing them the boost short-term profits (probably to justify bigger bonuses for the top dogs) with money that otherwise should have gone to shore up pension funds. And the hypocrisy continues, the worker is getting the short end of the stick. "The accounting is murky and needs a lot of attention," so says William Donaldson, chairman of the Securities and Exchange Commission. The past year's crackdown on corporate corruption has helped lure investors back to the stock market, but some companies still haven't grasped the importance of reform.

How can I trust an economic system that seems unable to fix its problems? What message is communicated to potential investors, some of whom were burned badly in the recent past by the corrupt practices of the investment community, when attracting them back to the stock market is described with the word "lure"? Are we considered too dumb to figure out the sucker-game that is being played?

Response:

Confidence in the integrity of those who lead us is essential. Perhaps we have been reading some of the same news stories. Mr. William Donaldson, head of the Securities and Exchange Commission, was recently speaking about the sweeping anti-fraud legislation enacted at the height of the scandals at Enron, WorldCom and other companies that wiped out billions in investors' savings. Almost in his next breath he acknowledged that there are still senior executives with greedy, yet seemingly legal, practices that risk the retirement savings of the rank and file.

Mr. Donaldson mentioned that companies (really, their leaders) must develop a new "moral DNA"—a culture that will last beyond the current management. Since when is ethical behavior new? Moral principles have been around since the time of Adam and Eve. Even though individuals may neglect to live by higher standards, there is no reason to act as if there were no guidelines. He mentioned that mutual fund companies should be required to make fuller disclosures of fees, which are too complicated for many consumers to understand. Once again, disclosure ought to be 100 percent open, clear and understandable. Basic integrity by those advising customers ought to be self-evident that the customer is to be served honestly. Do we really need federal and state laws to mandate straight talk?

He went on to suggest that investors should be told if their brokers have been given special inducements to sell particular mutual funds. What kind of investment advisor would not be forthcoming about conflicts of interest? Certainly an honest broker would be up front with any recommendations that grew from a personal agenda. Young people today have created a three-letter word that expresses my response to this comment: Duh! We are now learning that adults (individuals with credentials that communicate their qualifications to counsel others about managing money) need laws to make sure they behave decently. What is happening to us? Have we lost all sense of propriety and fair play?

As youngsters, about age 10, my pals and I would sometimes go fishing for the afternoon at one special small lake in southern Indiana. We had rods and reels and tackle boxes. We fished with worms and stink bait. We caught sunfish and crappies. But, when we wanted to impress one another, we raised up our casting rods and spinning rods so that we might connect to our line a special lure. This sure-fire fish magnet motivated us to cast for bass. We used different types of lures. Some danced on top of the water and others shone brightly as they moved erratically through the warm waters, often just below the surface. Our goal was to fool the fish and hook them on some artificial bait (a plastic device that appeared to be what it was not) and win the battle of wits with the fish. Sadly for me, most of the time, I couldn't get a bass to bite. When I did, it was victory and an accomplishment.

This is a great story if one is hooking a fish with a lure. It is a sad commentary, however, if those we need to trust with our life savings are hooking us with artificial promises (lures) so that they can take advantage of our lack of sophistication in the market and leave us with less than we started with while they "fee us into oblivion."

Bottom line for investing:

1. Make sure that you are comfortable building a relationship with

those who are to manage your money or offer you advice on your investments.

2. Be sure your investment resource has a track record of excellent earning performance.

3. Assess the advisor's "fit" with your values and priorities and refuse to compromise on anything that is important to you. Lawmakers cannot legislate behaviors that replace relationships. Regulations will not prevent frauds from stealing you blind.

4. Practice prudence and perseverance. Such discipline can go a long way in assessing performance.

5. Trust and verify, especially the values of those who might be helping you with your personal financial stewardship.

Unfortunately, hidden motives, driven by economic greed, can also place people's lives in jeopardy. Withholding information is even more reprehensible when it concerns issues of health (e.g., the effectiveness or potential harmful side effects of a particular medication or procedure). Like the telecommunications, accounting and energy industries, the health care industry has also been rocked by scandals. It can be argued that stock price, executive greed and corporate power games that centered on market share, played a role in the motivation to withhold information and risk lives.

Dear Jim:

On June 12, 2003, I learned from the media (newspapers and television) that Ancure, the heart surgery equipment maker, owned by Endovascular Technologies of Menlo Park, California, a subsidiary of Indianapolis-based Guidant Corporation, was charged with ten felony counts, including false statements to the Food and Drug Administration (FDA). The company was also charged with "fraudulent" sales of "misbranded" devices, again referring to the aneurysm stent-graft, known as the Ancure®.

The company was charged with two counts of failing to report as many as 2,600 malfunctions of the device, thus preventing the public and physicians from learning about "recurring malfunctions and other risks." The company is also accused of failing to report that other, more invasive operations were required after the device failed.

The criminal complaint alleges that the company misled the FDA and reported only 172 malfunctions since the product was introduced in 1999. The complaint alleges the company had records of 2,628 malfunctioning incidents, including reports that the malfunctions led to 12 deaths and 57 traditional open-heart surgeries.

How can we have confidence in medicine when things like this happen? Where is the level of integrity in the medical equipment manufacturing business?

Response:

This appears to be a horrible example of executive misconduct. To allow a flawed medical instrument to be placed in the hands of physicians and surgeons, after it was known to cause harm, is simply unacceptable. However, we must remain focused on the positive: Our free market system, supported by capitalism and guided by democracy, did discover the problem and it is being addressed. Prosecution in this situation will need to be thorough and swift.

Unfortunately, we know exactly why such events occur. Greed, whether for power or money (or both), is at the heart of this problem. Compromising health and life cannot be tolerated. Fortunately, such reckless endangerment seems to be the exception. Most manufacturers, and, especially the ones associated with health care, test and monitor each product to guarantee both quality and safety. Our society safeguards us with many agencies responsible for testing products that affect our lives. Organizations that we have created and support test, on our behalf, what we drive, wear, eat and utilize in all aspects of our lives, specifically in areas related to health care. These processes are overwhelmingly effective.

However, the utilization of the Ancure "stent-graft" device created troublesome and tragic results. We have been told that insiders of the firm, seemingly from the executive suites to the company's sales force who were present during "botched" surgical procedures, were participants in covering up the failures of the product. If the reports are accurate, then individuals in this firm were cheating with human lives. In contrast, cheating in competitive sports, as with a "corked bat" in the case of the famous Chicago Cubs baseball slugger, Sammy Sosa, disappointing as it may be, is nowhere in the league with risking human life just to sell a faulty heart device.

Some would argue that dishonesty is the same, whenever it occurs.

While saying that any dishonesty is the same—that any violation is terrible—may offer a grain of truth, this simplistic view obscures the multiple damages that this product and procedure has created. What we do know is that the Ancure "stent-graft" has caused continued and extraordinary pain for innocent patients, adding unnecessary suffering and cost as well as loss of earnings. How would you react if these same flawed surgical instruments, with instances of cover-up, had been used on one of your loved ones and precipitated a death? What if one of those affected was your mother or father, or a friend or loved one? And all you would have been able to do was watch helplessly, feeling frustration and disappointment that all too soon would turn into devastating grief.

It is too soon to know what will happen to this firm, its leadership and the reputation of medical manufacturing. What we do know is our judicial system is our best hope of creating justice for those who have been affected by this tragic series of events. When individuals compromise values for self-serving purposes, and lie about the safety or quality of the product they provide, then we are compelled to regulate their behavior, whether through prosecution and prison sentencing or increased governmental controls. Such violations of trust demand strong reactions.

The good news is that we have a self-regulating system. The bad news remains that some folks are still driven almost exclusively by greed and selfishness. And yet the very best part of the story is that we are allowed in our society to discuss such issues, publicly. Further, we must not lose sight of the promise of the free market system; namely, when free markets (including medical products manufacturers) regulate themselves, governments will not be required to do so. However, it appears in this instance, regulation to restore confidence and trust is required.

How much longer must we watch important leaders run amok before both we and they get the message? The masses of people are very willing to "give leaders a lot of freedom to solve problems," but there is a limit. When individuals in responsible positions (including medical equipment manufacturers) violate the trust of those they have promised to serve, then the buying public will react. As is our warning and caution to all who would violate basic integrity-centered commitments: "It should be common knowledge that free markets must regulate themselves or governments will." When the public trust is violated, and in this situation, with the potential for life and death consequences, then fear and anger will all to often replace confidence. The public (including those who have basic patients' rights) will ask for help that might easily support intrusive regulations, created by regulatory agencies, to correct the infractions.

Whether or not this is the right solution, it is a predictable response for individuals who have been wronged or believe they have been wronged. And, given the nature of our free market system, this may be the only legitimate long-term approach when individuals lose confidence that those in authority no longer operate with integrity-centered leadership and honesty. The time is now to restore honesty by rooting out the fraudulent.

Of course, rooting out the fraudulent can be especially difficult if one is an insider, subject to the coercive side of economic and hierarchical power. If an individual is aware of something wrong in his/her organization, there is risk associated with even raising the question, not to mention the disclosure of such information. This risk is well understood, and many companies have implemented anonymous ethics "hotlines." Providing safe and anonymous vehicles for well-meaning and caring employees to monitor corporate behavior has been the subject of legislation referred to as "whistleblower" laws. To date, such laws have been created to protect whistleblowers in the nuclear industry, the civil rights arena, the FBI and in other areas as well. In fact, as it pertains to federal government employees, agencies and departments, a federal employee is encouraged to file a complaint with the U.S. Office of Special Counsel. Even where such laws exist, the individual who is actually living in the situation may have concerns about subtle forms of retaliation, or even more subtle isolation over a length of time when it would be difficult to prove the connection between the disclosure and the retaliation

Disclosure of purpose by employees wishing to take time off for personal business is an area that has changed significantly as a result of the Internet and its potential. For decades, employees would inform employers when they needed to take time from the workplace to conduct important personal business—or even to do needed shopping. Today, personal business can often be transacted with a few quick "clicks" on a computer that has an Internet connection. Since this effort typically takes place right at the employee's work station, employers are less likely to be informed—and, in fact, many employers have become concerned that their employees are engaging in significant non-business activity on their workplace computers. Employers have had motivation to look into their employees' productivity, including computer activity. Every keystroke of a computer is saved in the machine's memory. Decision-makers may have chosen to look at every electronic message sent on their company e-mail server. Technology can track every website Universal Resource Locator (URL) and record all Internet sites an employee views. As discussed in the previous chapter, a person's Internet shopping can be tracked and recorded. Even when the computer memory is written over, some technologists can recover prior data. Employers who track employee activity may be viewed by some as "spying" on their employees, a violation of transparency, unless this practice is made known ahead of time. There is a real and practical need for openness in the way that companies treat their employees who have e-mail and Internet access. An "Integrity Matters" reader experienced exactly this issue, and presented it in the following question.

> Dear Jim:
>
> I just learned that my employer has been monitoring every Universal Resource Locator (URL) that I have visited on the Internet while at work. Of course, 99 percent of everything I do is for the company, but I have purchased books and DVD's online while at work. In the old days, I would take an hour of personal business and go to the store; now it takes me 10 minutes online. The company gains, but now they accuse me of using their time and computer resources inappropriately. What do you think? Am I violating integrity?

Response:

> Violating integrity depends, in part, on the contractual relationship you have with your company. Living and working with integrity also can be evaluated by the level of trust that exists between you and your company. Integrity can also be traced to the level and quality of your productivity for your company and the responsiveness and appreciation demonstrated by your company for your successful performance. After you answer these three questions, you will be clear about integrity concerns.
>
> First, what is your understanding of what you owe your employer in terms of measurable productivity? Do you know what your leader expects from you each and every day? Are you clear regarding how you are expected to utilize your workday? If you are unable to articulate answers to these questions, then gain that clarity, immediately.
>
> Second, do you have confidence that the leadership of your company, more precisely, your boss, has earned your trust and that you have earned both your supervisor's trust and the company's trust? Trust is the concrete

knowledge you have that integrity is at the center of transactions inside your company as well as with the outside world. Trust is the confidence that comes from the observation that behaviors expected throughout the organization are modeled by each and every leader. Unless or until this trust exists, there will always be an undercurrent of resentment and dissension that will erode openness and limit productivity.

Third, are you confident that you will be recognized and rewarded for going the extra mile as well as for consistency and dependability? At what point do you know for certain that excellent and consistent performance is the key to success in your organization? If you are assumed to be a partner in the organization, then there will be very little concern in how you take breaks and utilize those business tools for personal use. If, on the other hand, your every effort is under suspicion, then you can be confident that integrity and trust will not sustain the types of relationships required to build a healthy organization.

Now that you have answered questions about the company in these three areas, are you clear about the integrity issue? Now, just to make sure we have not overlooked the obvious, would your boss identify you as a productive partner or simply a paycheck earner? Are you simply one of the "slot fillers" who show up, giving only your time but not investing genuine commitment? Would your leadership team see you as an individual dedicated to corporate values or simply one who adheres to the rules when others are watching?

Trust is about the two-way relationship. Seek clarity regarding performance and work toward relationship and communications improvement so that you and your team members can build the atmosphere that nurtures openness, honesty, care and trust.

If you determine that this high quality of relationship exists and you are still monitored for every action you take, then you may want to rethink your evaluation or simply begin the process of looking for work elsewhere.

Of course, while we advocate openness and disclosure, we should not ignore the fact that many companies possess admirable histories, and have a tendency to do the right thing. Their values are built into their leadership cultures. We are reminded that, when a disgruntled individual injected poison into sealed bottles of Tylenol tablets many years ago, Johnson & Johnson reacted immediately, took all of this product off the shelves nationwide, and fully disclosed all of their actions to the public in a largely successful effort to maintain the trust it had worked hard to gain.

Corporations are structures that have the legal status of individuals, and function like people in that they have names, addresses and responsibilities. When the corporation or the individual is up front with goals and motivations, those who follow them do so with greater confidence. When communication is open, and not concealed, whether by design or by accident, morale and productivity tend to rise. To support openness, or transparency, corporations owned by the public are required to have annual meetings. At these meetings, stockholders can attend and vote on changes in their corporate charters, and elect directors to the board.

There are companies that hold these meetings in obscure locations away from major segments of stockholder population. These companies carefully stage and orchestrate the agenda so that incumbents on the board have little risk of challenge, and minority stockholder issues have little chance of a full hearing. In contrast, more responsive companies believe in transparency. These companies encourage stockholder participation, and the proceedings of their sessions are generally available to the public.

Annual meetings provide one more opportunity for leaders and organizations to confirm the importance of integrity-centered behavior in public companies. A case in point is addressed in the following exchange with a reader.

Dear Jim:

Forget about the corporate leadership scandals. Ignore the overly compensated executives. What about the trust that is required to get regular people to invest in companies? What about the trust that has been damaged by some of the same individuals exhibiting bad behavior? It has not been uncommon this past year for certain companies to hold their annual meetings in faraway places and allow "spokespersons" (such as hired outside attorneys) to do the talking. These official representatives are paid to handle all of the public communications, with little or no representation from either the board of directors or the executive team members themselves. We know this style of leadership is simply unproductive regarding the restoring of confidence and trust. These are not the kinds of companies in which I want to invest. Let them fall over the cliff if they don't clean up their acts.

But what about the thousands of other solid corporate leaders who have not been embarrassed by scandals or even been accused of being overly compensated; can their annual meetings restore trust? Please say yes! We need to find ways to strengthen the foundations of free markets. Can annual meetings help?

Response:

Yes, annual meetings can restore trust. Annual meetings can be powerful in areas related to motivation and confidence (trust) specifically when this type of tone is established:

1. Stockholders have appropriate access to the leader or leaders

2. The agenda is not so orchestrated that important content gets lost

3. Leaders own the problems and communicate sensible solutions to issues

4. Those in charge are willing to listen

5. Commitments are recorded and follow-up actions are systematically reviewed and evaluated in subsequent meetings and minutes

Unless or until such a tone is set, confidence in corporate leadership will not grow. Those who attend Berkshire Hathaway's annual shareholders' meeting, informed and inspired by Chairman Warren E. Buffett, generally walk away feeling that:

1. They have had genuine access to the leadership of the organization

2. Important issues are addressed in writing and discussed in person

3. Problems are identified, owned and addressed by those who are responsible, the boss or bosses, in this instance, Mr. Buffett

4. Concerns of individuals are heard, clearly and non-defensively

5. Responsive leadership fulfills promises, acknowledging any shortcomings along the way.

In a few words, ANNUAL MEETINGS CAN RESTORE TRUST when the leaders who structure and conduct them work on a model that operates along lines similar to those of Berkshire Hathaway's. As a mentor of mine was quick to say: "There is no substitute for the truth." Yes, integrity matters. Tell the truth and demand the truth, all the time.

Each of us has a responsibility to leave the world better than we found it. It is time that we make the commitment, a plan for our lives, and hold it in highest esteem, to restore integrity through insight. It is easy and fashionable to point to the flaws of corporate leadership. Millions of supporters of the "bash business brigade" are ready and willing to join the chorus of criticism. There are legitimate reasons to hold high-powered leaders' feet to the fire. However, if we stop there, we may have missed an opportunity to make a really big difference. By going just one step further, we might change society.

Most of us know right from wrong. We know what excesses are, whether in executive pay, driving too fast, drinking too much, abusing drugs, cheating on marriage, lying on taxes or ignoring children. Our behaviors sometimes give us away. While we are quick to pull the trigger on shooting down the big shots for their errors, there is a really good chance millions of others would too often trade the ease of our own "rule violations" for the right to "look the other way" when those all around want a little latitude in bending and breaking laws and traditions. And we know this is wrong. We cannot inspire the next generation positively and constructively with this operating style. We must first face ourselves and then decide that appropriate changes can begin when individuals start looking in the mirror and facing an honest reflection of behavior.

In our various activities, it is appropriate that we demand, through our personal and professional priorities, "a world in which people do what they say, are forthright in their communications, and a handshake solidifies any promise." Such a commitment would underscore that integrity matters, first in day-to-day matters and ultimately in all transactions. Since each of us is Chief Executive Officer (CEO) of ourselves, then every encounter of our life is a meeting. These daily transactions are similar to a larger corporation's annual meeting. How we conduct our business and personal relationships can build or tear down trust. So, on a personal level, integrity will flourish and trust will grow when individuals (small corporations of ourselves) conduct themselves with:

1. An availability and an ease with others

2. A tone that invites give-and-take and encourages new ideas

3. Courage and accountability in facing problems; graciousness in handling success

4. An atmosphere of openness and receptivity

5. Tenacious and timely follow-through.

The time to restore trust is now. Are you willing to begin the process?

Building a climate of trust requires transparency, so that stakeholders never have to say, "I wonder what they are up to this time?" Openness, or transparency, is essential to healthy relationships—for parents, educators, spiritual leaders, government employees, role models and bosses. Openness is an important assurance that a Chief Executive Officer can build into the organization. to discourage greed from corrupting the mission.

Perhaps equally important, the word of a trusted company is accepted, and therefore its decisions, recruiting and product statements are believed. The company that is trusted will be significantly more profitable over time, other things being equal. The authority of its integrity-centered reputation is strengthened, a subject to be addressed in the following chapter.

Chapter 7

AUTHORITY:
Employee Encouragement

... you don't make decisions because they are easy;
you don't make them because they are cheap;
you don't make them because they're popular;
you make them because they're right.
– Theodore M. Hesburgh

"Authority" can refer to a person, as in "She is an authority on that subject." It may be an attribute, as in "He has the authority." It could refer to an organization, such as "the Port Authority." Confining the scope of authority to only that of a person with a vested position in an organization's hierarchy is too narrow. Because we speak of "the voice of authority" or of a person as "an authority on the subject," we know that positional authority is not the only kind. An individual exercising authority based only upon the power of a title may compel just the minimum level of performance. However, when those who follow instructions and directives feel engaged by leaders who encourage individual dignity, productivity levels are likely to be excellent.

The issue of authority is illustrated in a story of a production manager whose factory was behind schedule on an important project. The production manager went to the floor and demanded that the supervisor tell him why the schedule was not being met. As the supervisor began to explain the overtime and process changes needed to regain the schedule, the production manager interrupted and shouted, "I don't need excuses, I need results!" He ordered the first-line supervisor to meet the schedule without the additional resources and changes, yelling, "Just get it done!" The supervisor calmly suggested that the two of them sit down in a conference room to go over what would be needed, whereupon the production manager exclaimed, "Who do you think runs things around here?" The supervisor said, "I guess you do," and handed him the clipboard and returned to his seat, whereupon the workers watching this exchange simply sat back and waited. The production manager had no idea where to begin to recover without the supervisor, so he said, "Stop staring and get back to work!" The workers turned around, but with a questionable level of effort, and with knowing looks exchanged along the assembly line.

The production manager of course had the higher position, but the people had respect for the knowledge and track record of the supervisor, and their collective silence more than offset the positional authority of the "big boss."

Generally speaking, authority is the ability to make other people do what you want them to do, and is basically of two kinds: power and influence. People in leadership positions fall back on power when they lack the influence to persuade people to follow them; this is the weakest form of persuasion. Power is derived from physical strength, the law, economic resources and hierarchical position. Its strength lies in the ability to compel people to do what they may not wish to do, because of a coercive condition—the ability to injure, to damage the follower economically, to withhold favor, or to restrain the freedom of the follower. Its difficulty lies in the simple condition that whether or not he or she wants to, the follower must follow—or else. In this case, he or she is unlikely to produce the highest level of energy and focus in the face of such power, and, indeed, may not be able to.

Influence power, on the other hand, is the ability to bring people to conclude that they want to follow the leader. It may be derived from knowledge, reputation or prior relationships. Influence power may be acquired by demonstrated courage, as many battlefield leadership stories have shown. If a leader has superior knowledge and can demonstrate this with persuasive skills, then, using such knowledge, he or she will likely cause the follower to respond appropriately. Similarly, if a would-be leader enters the transaction with a respected reputation, others will be inclined to follow. The influence position of a personal relationship is simply this: People who feel a bond toward the would-be leader will be inclined to follow, in support of continuing the bond. Where knowledge, reputation and relationship are all present in the leader, then that individual can harness the followers' capabilities, excitement and energy, which are likely to be given freely.

Both forms of authority can be vested in an individual leader, of course, and they can also be vested in leadership teams, in organizations and in industries. Directors of a public company (itself a leadership team) have the authority of their position in dealing with the company officers, and have the potential to develop influence authority over the investor as they behave wisely over time. An example of this is the space industry, which possesses the leading edge of technical knowledge, the excitement of exploration as well as ground-floor opportunities for bright and ambitious people. These combined factors generate the energy level required for maximum performance. Similarly, the International Red Cross has a certain amount of position authority (granted by governments) to act during disasters; it acquires influence authority as it behaves responsibly during such emergencies. Another example is the petroleum industry, which has position authority over the pricing and distribution of needed products such as gasoline and heating oil, and it has the opportunity to gain influence authority both through its knowledge of petroleum characteristics and through its behavior in times of shortage.

In the context of integrity, "authority" largely refers to the ability to influence others. If a company or an individual leader is to be regarded as having integrity, then that entity or person either must possess an appropriate level of knowledge or have earned respect for past behavior in acquiring such a reputation for consistent and appropriate behavior. Relationships must be handled in a manner that generates respect. Such authority inspires followers to such an extent that they are motivated to give their maximum level of performance; a level of focused energy that is unavailable to them when they are not so encouraged. Consider how much energy a person has when he or she is in a situation that is forced and not desirable; compare that to the level and quality of energy a person has when pursuing something that is desirable (at a time, place and means of his or her own choosing).

The ability to influence others is often used in the service of a person's career, and that authority can be exercised with varying degrees of responsibility. The following exchange regarding the life of newscaster David Brinkley presents an example of influence authority that many would agree was used constructively.

> Dear Jim:
>
> David Brinkley was a pioneer of the news media. In his own words, "I was at NBC when the first television camera was rolled in. So I've been around a long time. I am one of the pioneers. I guess I've become part of the wallpaper in this country."
>
> David Brinkley and his co-anchor at NBC News, Chet Huntley, garnered fame far beyond the realm of journalism. In 1965, a consumer-research company found that Huntley and Brinkley were recognized by more adult Americans than John Wayne or The Beatles.
>
> Did David Brinkley represent integrity? Was his integrity what caused him to be so admired?

Response:

America, with the death of David Brinkley on June 11, 2003, has lost a superstar. David Brinkley, pioneer of the press, communicated a sense of proportion about his work and himself. He seemed to be comfortable reporting the news with no effort on his part to become the news. Whether he was liberal or conservative, he delivered his reporting in an evenhanded manner. When he did choose to make his opinions known, he offered them straight out, direct, to the point and seemingly, without appearing vindictive or needing to apologize.

David Brinkley would not be a "spin doctor," nor would he have hired one. He called them as he saw them. For that reason alone, one could describe him as an individual with integrity; precisely because with Brinkley there was congruence between what he said and what he did, as well as what he said about what he did. His honesty could be felt, from his words and his "on-camera" delivery. At least, that was how he appeared for about 60 years. Faking integrity for six decades is difficult, if not impossible, especially when millions of people are watching and listening, day in and day out.

It could be that his celebrity and fame were the result of a less complicated time. The era in which he built his career, from the 1940's to 1990's, was moving toward (but had not yet achieved) current levels of cynicism and mistrust of public figures. In the heyday of his successes, reporters were the sources of important information. News broadcasting had not yet sunk to more recent greed-driven levels with the "take no prisoners" pursuit of ratings and revenues. It appeared the pioneers were not willing to trade substance for sound bites and sensationalism.

In the early days of television journalism, news professionals such as Brinkley, Edward R. Murrow and Walter Cronkite recognized the importance of honesty, courage and forthrightness. The public placed its trust in them and they knew it. Network anchors did not come on other broadcasts with "teasers" about stories they would be discussing on their own upcoming news shows. Such obvious advertising and marketing by news reporting leaders would have been seen as inappropriate, even cheap. David Brinkley stood above such self-serving and mercenary behavior. His work was to provide important information to his viewers who had confidence that he would not let them down.

So, what is it about David Brinkley's death that causes us to pause and reflect?

First, we yearn for times when trust and integrity were the currency of the day.

Second, we know that such courage and predictability will be hard to replace.

Third, his death is a signal that we must not continue the mindless feeding of an insatiable appetite for the sensational at the expense of the important, no matter the financial incentives.

Fourth, his life reminds us that we are stewards of integrity and each time we compromise it for short-term recognition and ego satisfaction, we put our values at risk.

Fifth, we have finally lost his steadiness as well as his presence, at the wheel of the great ship called "television news broadcasting" and we will never again hear his thoughtful, integrity-centered comments nor feel his reassuring stature as he signs off at the end of a thoughtful and substantive television broadcast.

Brinkley appears to have retained his integrity, remained a trusted news broadcaster while becoming an icon in the news arena because his influence authority never waned. Clearly, David Brinkley held enormous influence authority that went beyond the television community, and his death is a substantial loss.

The authority of influence can be lost or reduced by the erosion of the reputation of the would-be leader, company or industry. Another way to damage authority is to violate relationships with followers and colleagues. Influence can be lost when the expert is found wrong in his or her area of expertise, the religious leader is found to have committed a moral error, the professional athlete is found to have used performance-enhancing substances, or the company with a pristine image is found to have committed fraud. Sometimes this process occurs incrementally over time, and sometimes it can happen with the rush of immediate events.

The following letter provides an illustration that may be common, and in which an executive's moral authority is damaged without any direct, career-destroying, side effect (at least not in the short term).

Dear Jim:

I work for an executive who has always been held in high esteem, but just recently he submitted an expense item for me to OK for reimbursement, that I believe to be personal. This involved an expensive dinner with friends and for which there was no business purpose, not even relationship-building, as their personal friendship is well-established. Of course, he could and no doubt would justify it as a legitimate business expense if challenged, and my push back would be seen as a complaint. Chances are that the conversation between us would not yield any results other than irritation for everyone concerned.

Response:

When someone who has been held in high esteem disappoints us, it is natural to feel disappointment, sometimes even anger. When we perceive that our values, small or large, are violated, one or both of the parties involved can feel a tear in the relationship-fabric of mutual faith and confidence. The breaking of a trust, in this instance, the inappropriate use of company funds, can signal that a halo of an individual with perceived integrity was tarnished. Casual or irresponsible behavior about what is and what is not a proper use of a business expense account can shatter an otherwise worthy reputation. It sounds as if your role in the company places you in a position to exercise your fiduciary responsibility for the conduct of others, even some who are held in high esteem.

You have determined that this individual has exercised poor judgment. Without knowing your area of responsibility, it sounds as if you are simply carrying out tasks related to your job. You are sensitive to wasting money, at any level and for any reason. You are looking out for the stockholders' interests who expect responsible management to be good stewards of their investment dollars. Further, without profits and proper cash flow, financial abuses will lower profits and risk the jobs of fellow employees. Casual business behaviors are seldom wise and they can be devastating in financial areas, whether on the income or expense side.

But, let's get back to your dilemma. What is the integrity-centered action in this instance? First, let's check this situation carefully. In general, I've found it helpful to view such matters as isolated incidents from this perspective:

If it happens once, it is an event. If it happens twice, it is a pattern. If it happens a third time, it is a habit, and habits are very hard to break.

If the executive in question has not been sloppy with expenses before, then it may be prudent to ask if this expense item was an oversight. If the leader's "halo" is still in place and you are correct that the meal should not be charged to the company, then mentioning the issue should allow the other person, and not you, to rectify the error. Sometimes a simple question, "Did you mean to do this?" will remind the executive that he or she lives in a fishbowl, and that their behavior is being observed and emulated. As a consequence, leaders' behaviors are open to question, if only for clarification. With a basically honorable person, such a reminder will be sufficient. Their response will also tell you a great deal about whether this was an incident, a pattern or a habit. If the executive's behavior is habitual, you will want to extricate yourself from that situation. Sooner or later, habitual abusers of funds, small or large, will do harm to the enterprise. They will create enough distrust that increased regulations will be required and new rules will relationships and stifle motivation. Integrity matters 24 hours a day, 7 days a week. Leaders are role models, for better or worse, on purpose or by accident.

Another type of moral authority was eroded by the frailties of self-proclaimed role models, most obvious in the scandals associated with television ministries. When some of these electronic powerhouses were found guilty of misbehavior, their influence and message were jeopardized; the authority they had enjoyed was dramatically impacted. Some lost their lucrative television pulpits, and at least one person served time in prison. Followers, believers and contributors must have felt violated.

There are those who attempt to make a distinction between a person's ethical behavior as a corporate executive and his or her ethical behavior as a private person. Each of us is but one and the same individual, and the damage done in one arena will detract from influence authority in the other. But time can resolve serious issues. If we are to rebuild the trust within our society, we must first begin with the individual, personally, then allow that character and strength to be reflected in a professional leadership role.

Sometimes the loss of influence authority is sudden, total and shocking; this is often associated with criminal activity. One of our readers asked a question concerning the total loss of influence authority by the leader of a nonprofit organization.

Dear Jim:

On June 14, 2003, the following was printed in *The San Jose Mercury News*: "The head of a charity that once claimed to have brought Croatian children to the United States stood in handcuffs Friday in a Palo Alto courthouse. [The accused] faces allegations that she scammed the Italian family of a 6-year-old with leukemia by making false promises she would get them medical help at Stanford. The girl eventually died."

What has happened to integrity? How can we allow innocent children to be victimized by such individuals?

Response:

First, you are on target with your concern. We must never ignore social abuses, especially destructive activities impacting children who are unable to protect themselves. The situation you described is horrible. There is no integrity when scam artists raise hopes for critically needed medical services that will not be delivered. Lowlife crooks will take money from anyone, including financially strapped families. They prey on unsuspecting parents who believe their investment will resolve a health crisis for their child.

Fortunately, such dishonest behavior is still the exception. But when it happens to those less able to cope with these damages, righteous indignation becomes justifiable anger. We cannot tolerate big bullies (liars, cheats and frauds who take money under false pretenses) beating up on, and taking advantage of, weaker individuals (in this situation, literally, sick children with desperate parents in a seemingly helpless dilemma).

Second, integrity is alive or your sense of outrage would not be evident, as it is from your questions. Obviously, human values were nurtured in you by your family during your formative years, and you have maintained a social consciousness. You care. We all should. Your outrage can be a source of reassurance for those reading this column. Integrity in relationships, medical care standing at the very top, must never be compromised.

Third, we must continue to learn intelligent ways to navigate the complex roads of life. When my father passed along wisdom to me, it was often in the form of personal stories. One of his illustrations responds directly to your concern about ways nasty people victimize others. Twenty-four years ago, during my first months of not very successfully launching a new business, Dimension Five Consultants, Inc., my father was listening to me describe a long list of disappointing meetings with potential clients.

We had talked long enough that the telephone actually felt hot against the side of my head. One person after another had made a promise, only to let me down; not returning calls, failing to meet with me as promised and refusing to fulfill promises they had made to utilize my consulting services. My fear of failure gave way to dismay. These powerful individuals, in responsible positions, were behaving badly. How could that be? Then I offered my question: "But, Dad, you said that cream rises to the top. And these people are pretty high up in companies. Why is it that they are not acting like the top-quality human beings?" Then came the long fatherly pause.

"Son, you have no experience on a farm. You see, when I was a young man, often I was up early in the morning milking cows. And, yes, the cream did rise to the top. However, when we made our way from the cow, milk bucket in hand, to the separator, and just before we poured off the cream, we were always careful to scrape away the ring of scum that rested at the very top of the cream." The second long period of silence followed. (I was supposed to figure this out, this lesson in cream, milk and scum. But, fortunately, the fatherly interpretation was soon to be presented as a lesson in practical application.)

Fourth, my father offered this guidance: "Whether it is separating cream and milk from the scum or distinguishing top leadership from the pretenders masquerading as power brokers, it is always wise to remember that upon first glance, differences may be difficult to discover. Be patient. Ask for second opinions. Never assume that money, power or prestige guarantees either quality or integrity. Be careful before drawing conclusions based solely upon appearances."

Fifth and finally, we know down deep that to save the lives of children, we must continue to monitor the reckless and criminal behaviors of those who make false promises and destroy lives. Our justice system will remain vigilant to these crimes. Scum, so it seems, will always be there and we are challenged to remove it before it sours the cream that is the best of who we are and what we can provide.

When any individual violates a promise—stated or implied—whether for profit or charity, integrity suffers along with reputation and authority.

Leadership reputations can be constructed or eroded by the behavior of senior management. The question and response that follows is an example of a businessperson engaging in behavior that is ultimately described as "chiseling." One can imagine that people employed by this person would form a very clear image of this individual, and would almost certainly view their own compensation and benefits as being subject to this counterproductive behavior and the attitude that informs it.

Dear Jim:

A businessman that I know charges his retail customers for priority mail postage—as though it were a reimbursement for his costs—but then collects a refund from the Post Office whenever they fail to meet the delivery schedule—which happens a lot. In effect, this businessman has another source of revenue—reimbursed fees that were subsequently refunded by the Post Office, because he never passes the refund on to the customer. Is this right? Does this action have integrity?

Response:

As a youngster, growing up in the Midwest, small-town Indiana, there was an expression, actually a word, used to describe such behavior. The word described individuals who were on the borderline of what was legal and moral. They may have been unscrupulous or maybe just greedy. They knew every way imaginable to cut a corner, save a buck, take advantage of any opportunity and they were not above pushing their way to the front of the line at the county fair just to get a corn dog and a root beer. They were so low that other people knew about the time they returned a half-eaten box of cookies to the grocer claiming they found something wrong with the carton and the taste of the cookies.

These were the folks who complained loudly in restaurants and often ate for free or for a reduced price. Their focus on every nickel and dime was so extreme that some called them tight and others described them as cheap. But the one term that always stuck in my memory was much more descriptive. It gathered the force of resentment that can only described as suitable for selfish and nasty personalities. It was a word that none of my friends and I ever wanted used to portray who we were or how we operated. This hideous term smelled of smoked-filled rooms where questionable deals might be completed. It smacked of corruption. And, always the word carried with it a tone of rudeness and ruthlessness.

Later in my life, after living in Missouri, Illinois, Connecticut and then California, I would be reassured that there was no doubt the term had been accurate. Even in friendly games of cards, horseshoes, checkers or golf, this type of a person exists to do one thing, over and over: take advantage of every occasion and where possible, to cheat. These kinds of people have only one objective, whether for a few pennies or dollars, and that is to take advantage of others and win at all costs. These people even play dirty at the famous board game of Monopoly. Sometimes people of this kind will hide the "Get Out of Jail Free" card (sometimes underneath their pile of play money) and spring it on you when they roll the dice that is supposed to land them in jail, where the rules say that they must lose a turn. And that is when they remember they have the "jail pass," just so they won't miss even one more opportunity to win the game. They are beneath any level of basic niceness. These individuals are hucksters; that's right, HUCKSTERS. In more polite circles, one might call them by different terms like foxy, clever, prudent, calculating, competitive or shrewd. The truth is they are hucksters.

One hopes that their ill-gotten dollars, which sometimes have led them to fame and recognition, will enable them to "buy" enough friends to hang around so they will have a social life when they are old, rich and often peering through their squinty-eyed bitterness.

People who gouge others in the way you described this "postage fraud" of an acquaintance only confirm that he is truly a huckster. We were advised as children to watch out for hucksters because they target just about everyone with whom they come in contact. Be careful. Folks like this can all too easily ignore integrity because they have forgotten that integrity matters.

Were an employee to be asked by this businessperson to emulate this "chiseling" behavior, it would amount to an abuse of authority. An abuse of authority arises when management puts someone into a position where they are expected to do something that they would not otherwise do, a violation of their own values, and which is a restriction on their personal freedom. Sometimes an abuse is obvious, as in the demand to change a time card, or being asked to look the other way while the boss takes home company-owned materials such as office supplies, food or lumber. Other abuses can be more subtle, as is demonstrated by the situation described in the following letter.

Dear Jim:

My company is involved in a Political Action Committee (PAC). I would rather control my own contributions. Each time the senior team meets lately, the Chief Executive Officer goes around the table and reports who has contributed what to date. He then "encourages" his direct reporting staff to get all their people "on board." I am feeling pressure to contribute when I do not want to. What should I do?

Response:

In some corporate circles this behavior must be commonplace. Perhaps large salaries are provided with an unspoken expectation that some of these dollars are to be "made available" for the candidates chosen by the leadership team.

Companies have a legitimate interest in focusing Political Action Committee contributions to those candidates whose philosophy and/or voting history is favorable to the vested interests of that company, and also have the privilege to expect managers to be loyal to the "management views" of the organization.

A problem can arise when employees feel that contributions are virtually forced at some level by their management. This seems to be the issue you are raising here.

Assuming these "expectations" are legal, then you still have choices to make. Participate at the level you deem adequate or look for a different organization to join. If your frustration and resentment "bubble over" into your day-to-day transactions and become counterproductive, your reputation in the organization will suffer. It is your own reputation and career that are at risk.

Intimidation seldom fosters a healthy environment, regardless of the motive. Clearly, the problem is the implied coercion, and not the earmarking of contributions, which has become part of our system for funding political activities. Employees, whether in management or in individual contributing positions, are well-advised to understand the policies, both written and unwritten, that exist in their organization. "Acceptable behavior" can be—and often is—defined differently by different companies. Policies can range from a company's dress code to its customer service philosophy. Communication is key in making sure all members of the organization are informed of those policies, so their behavior will reflect them. But what happens when an employee does what he or she believes to be the right thing, and is subsequently disciplined for acting in opposition to company policy? The following is an example of what can happen when a supervisor (someone who has authority over an employee) fails to communicate company policy clearly. Part of the responsibility for the miscommunication is the employee's, however; she possibly could have prevented this misunderstanding by asking the supervisor for clarification.

Dear Jim:

Last year, when I graduated from -a local community college, I got a job at a local clothing store. After some initial training I was put on the sales floor. I enjoyed the work. I like taking care of people's needs.

Although I wasn't getting much feedback from my manager, I thought I was doing a pretty good job. Customers were always thanking me for the way I helped them. Then, last week, I was suddenly fired over an incident that has left me hurt and confused.

A lady had come into the store looking for a particular brand of cotton top. We didn't carry the brand or anything else similar in style. I knew that a shop in the mall had what she was looking for and so I told her where she could find what she wanted. I then asked if she had seen our sale items or if I could help her in any other way. She said she was just interested in the blouses, thanked me and left.

My manager, who had overheard my conversation with the lady, came up to me and told me she wanted to see me in the break room after my shift. Two hours later, before I was going to punch out, I went to see the manager. To my shock, when I met the manager she handed me my final check and told me I was being let go effective immediately. I will never forget her words when I asked her why. She said, "You never, ever, refer a customer to a competitor." I was so stunned. I don't even remember what I said in my defense. I just remember leaving the store a nervous wreck.

Is it possible that general business practices say that self-interest comes before the best interest of the customer? Please tell me this isn't so.

Response:

This should not have happened, yet it provides a lesson: Simply being right is no guarantee that we will not have some "bumps." As to your boss, everyone understands that these are demanding times. Generating revenue is tough. Likely, your former boss was feeling tremendous pressure to generate immediate cash flow from customers, despite not having exactly what the customer wanted or needed. Unless your former boss had instructed you that you were never to refer a customer to another supplier to fulfill their needs (a poor policy, by the way), your boss was wrong to terminate you for this. From a customer's perspective, you made the right decision and are living with the consequences.

When your own integrity is on the line, there is a piece of wisdom that you might choose to read, over and over. It appears on our Website (www.brachercenter.com): "Integrity is one of several paths; it distinguishes itself from the others because it is the right path and the only one upon which you will never get lost." — M.H. McKee

You chose to meet a customer's needs by telling him or her the truth. You maintained your personal integrity and might possibly have created a customer for life for your former employer. Shortsighted bosses, those who are driven only by today's profits at the expense of longer-term relationships, are not the "stuff" of which legends have been built. They miss opportunities to create legendary service by focusing exclusively upon today's financial results. Bosses of this type terminate individuals of your caliber. Long term, businesses that operate this way lose out. Longer term, please be confident that you will win—as will the many customers that you will continue to attract and retain.

You are now in a very good position (having encountered a shortsighted, self-centered and greedy boss) to look with greater precision for the integrity-centered leader and organization that will respect and reward your focus on the customer. Most of the time, with the majority of people, integrity is important. Being honest is rewarded. Good leaders are working hard to equip each of their employees so that every individual will feel comfortable doing the right thing for the right reasons.

You have learned that one particular organization is not a good match for you. Be happy that you have learned this so soon upon graduation. You are now better prepared to proceed with confidence that high integrity situations do exist which will welcome you, promote you and regard you as true partner in their efforts to serve the customers effectively.

This supervisor used her own position power and authority to defend selfish and shortsighted policies. Her position made it possible for this insensitive, harsh firing to happen. In this instance, who really wins? No one. It is likely that the terminated employee will have told family, friends and future employers about this experience, to the detriment of the supervisor and the business involved. That is the nature of influence authority; it can be positive or negative.

An example of the beneficial use of influence authority that bridges both family and work life can be seen the following story.

One pre-dawn morning in the springtime a few years ago, a traveler found himself sitting high up in the shoe-shine booth of an airport, reading a newspaper while his shoes were being cleaned and polished. A casual question, "What's new?" to the shoe shiner, generated an intriguing response: "Don't ever steal anything small!" This statement was followed by an avalanche of insights.

The traveler put down his newspaper and asked for further explanation. "For starters," the shoe shiner said, looking up at the wide-eyed customer, "if you get caught stealing something small, you are most likely going to be sent to a really tough prison. However, if you are convicted of taking something big, lots of money for example, you will end up in a better facility, something more like a country club." The speaker knew about legal issue; his son was a corporate attorney and his grandson was in his final year of law school. This hardworking grandfather described their successes with great pride.

The story picked up several more times during the following six months, culminating in the customer learning that #1 grandson had also been recognized by his East Coast law school, earning top honors. The beaming shoe shiner even shared a photograph of the extended family taken during his grandson's commencement.

Within three generations, life had changed tremendously for this family. The shoe shiner was very clear that he had asked for government assistance to help pay for his son's education, but had never sought further support. He appreciated what the system had made available, and felt others, not him or his family, deserved a similar boost. He used his authority position as the family patriarch to demonstrate self-sufficiency, positively influencing both his son and grandson. Here is a living, life-changing example of how the responsible exercise of authority can create opportunities for future generations. A legacy of this caliber is priceless; it cannot be purchased for any amount of money. It must be lived.

As was the case with the hardworking grandfather whose values and priorities created unbelievable opportunities for his son and his grandchildren, so it is with integrity-centered relationships. The interpersonal connections that tie responsible parents to children are similar to those binding values that strengthen productive relationships between and among employers and employees.

Organizations with integrity, and leaders with integrity, exercise their position authority with care and restraint. Wise and effective leaders rely instead on the authority of influence, which emerges from relationships built on trust and respect. The ability to persuade, to inspire and to encourage—now, that is integrity-centered authority!

Chapter 8

PARTNERSHIP:
Honor Obligations

Associate with [individuals] of good quality
if you esteem your own reputation;
for it is better to be alone than in bad company.
– George Washington

No matter how success is defined, it is seldom accomplished alone. Learning requires the help of another. To achieve a relationship requires, obviously, the participation of another. For joint progress to be made among individuals, cooperation—teamwork—is needed among the participants. To achieve economic success clearly requires a structure of exchange in which others play a role. Manufacturers need both raw materials and customers.

We are engaged, then, in a variety of partnerships. A person of integrity recognizes that most relationships involve partnership, wherein each party realizes that the needs of the other must be satisfied if the relationship is to continue. Violations of trust, however small, can threaten the health of any relationship. In order to restore trust within society by becoming self-regulating (thereby minimizing the need for government regulatory involvement), we must work together to sustain relationships by honoring obligations, both personal and professional. We need to be responsible partners.

We know that the leader with integrity works to satisfy not only the needs of his or her organization, but also the needs of suppliers, donors, customers, employees and other stakeholders. This makes sense; it is just good business. If a long-term relationship is to survive and prosper, then the commitments of an individual and an organization must be trustworthy and reliable. Promises must be kept.

Restoring trust begins with the individual. Trust grows when all parties concerned do what they say they are going to do and engage in integrity-centered behaviors. Expectations must be made clear, and violations corrected. As leaders engage in integrity-centered behaviors, their relationships improve. As relationships work better, the organizations tend to also work better. Trust is thus restored, one behavior at a time, one partnership at a time.

Partnership impact begins in the home. The basic structure of human society, clearly, is the family. Accordingly, if we are to strengthen integrity-centered behavior in our society, we must begin with the behavior of the individual in the family setting. A strong partnership must be maintained between husband and wife in the management and leadership of the household. Again, trustworthiness and reliability are important elements in any type of partnership, but especially so between family members whose well-being and existence are to some degree dependent on the quality of the partnerships established between the individuals. The following exchange represents an overarching concern about the role of honoring obligations with regard to the family.

> Dear Jim:
>
> When are we going to get serious about keeping promises to our children? Our marriages? Our values? Our societies? Isn't it time we start keeping our promises?

> Response:
>
> Yes, it is time to address promises. We make them all the time. We can help to rebuild the moral tone of our society. We demonstrate our promise keeping when we show up on time (or even early). We honor promises when we listen attentively and not judgmentally.
>
> We keep promises when we work for the pay we take. We keep promises when we nurture children, ours and those of others. We keep promises when we encourage others to "try," and congratulate them when they address disappointment appropriately.
>
> We keep promises when we thank those who have helped us. Promise making and promise keeping are the foundation of trust, respect, dignity, autonomy and relationship.
>
> Make a list of your promises: made and kept. If they fail to match up, retrace your steps and fulfill the unfilled commitments. Sometimes the "magic" words are no more complicated than saying "please," "thank you," "I am sorry," "I made a mistake."

But important relationships are kept together and made strong by more than promises. Partnership in a family, for example, requires each participant to be aware of the needs of the other; anticipating, reaching out and intervening when necessary, as is demonstrated by the following letter.

Dear Jim:

I am frightened. Recently my husband returned from one of several long business trips. He has never been under such pressure to sell products, raise capital and keep his board happy. We talk, as we have for the 29 years we have been married. He considers me his best friend and sounding board. So, this is what scares me.

We were talking about his job, where he is the president, and he said that things were rough, so rough that he hopes he is dead before they ever get this rough again. What can I say or do to help him?

Response:

Now, more than ever, we need our friends and loved ones. It is their understanding and support that will sustain us. Your husband sounds overwhelmed, and why not? These are rough times. Keep the doors of communication open. Continue to listen. If this is a one-time conversation, the listening may be all that is needed. If the conversations continue over an extended time so that it is clear the conditions are not temporary, then help him plan an exit to a healthier situation. Life is short! Handle with care.

This relationship between immediate family members is intended, as shown above, to be one of mutual support; yet there is an art form in knowing when to listen and when to attempt an intervention, hoping to change and improve the circumstances. There is a powerful reminder that parents, in their integrity-centered partnership with their children, are to provide wings for freedom and a sure foundation for stability. Whether as spouse, parent, friend or co-worker, the mandate seems to apply. Kites that fly the highest have the strongest connecting line, enabling the hard winds of resistance to propel the kite, as well as the individual, to achieve the greatest heights.

Dear Jim:

Three months ago my wife came home from a "Business Opportunity Meeting" she was invited to by someone at our church, and she was very excited. She said that a couple of people who spoke at the meeting were showing off checks for over $25,000 that they had received in monthly bonuses for putting together sales organizations selling vitamins and herbs. No matter how much I told my wife that this sounded like some kind of shady pyramid scheme, she said we could use the extra money and she was "going for it."

So far, after spending $700 on product and training materials, she has made a grand total of $140 in commissions. More troubling is that my wife has gotten many of our friends and relatives into her little enterprise. I think she has too much pride to admit she's been had by visions of "striking it rich." She still insists that, with more time and by recruiting even more friends and relatives, she will start making big money. I'm worried that the only thing we're going to end up with is a bunch of damaged relationships from the people my wife has encouraged to join her business crusade.

Is there any chance that my wife's business can pan out? Should I force her to give this up before any more money and time are thrown away?

Response:

Obviously, you love your wife, care about your friends and are concerned that your wife's business skills may not match the needs of the enterprise. Losing any of the above can be costly. Therefore, ask your wife if she is motivated by the mission of her new enterprise or by its promise of dollars.

Also, you ask if you should "force her to give this up," and this gives rise to a different caution: A marriage is often understood to be a partnership, in which each partner brings something to the relationship in return for mutual support and the contribution of the other partner. If you imagine that you can "force" your partner to do something, then it is unlikely that you have the kind of partnership we describe in other discussions. Perhaps it was your choice of terms, when what you meant was to influence with enthusiasm. Either way, partnerships are precious, business and marital.

In all likelihood, then, your wife needs to make her own decisions—so you help best by asking her the right focus questions.

Generally, among the successful people I know, all know [that] profits are the by-product and not the goal. If the product or service is good, it will sell, assuming it is properly capitalized, marketed and supported. Most business owners, such as your wife, develop a budget and set of milestones for the enterprise and once the investment capital is exhausted, they decide to dig deeper or say "enough" and close the doors, depending upon progress against the milestones. Check the company. Check your wife's plan. What results are being achieved against expectations for this point in time? Be open about the budget. Make the decision together. Then, move on. Integrity is then maintained, personally and professionally, as partners.

Clearly, then, the partnership of the family, including parents and children, is ideally a relationship between and among concerned stakeholders, each with a different position and perspective. Indeed, the maturing process of children will benefit from a form of partnership between the parents and the child wherein each understands, appreciates and accommodates the role of the other. Parents who view their role as a nurturing, teaching and supportive one will more likely develop a healthy partnership with the child. In contrast, a parent who does not partner in this way may view his or her role only from the standpoint of judgment, control and correction, which can easily become adversarial. The concept of honoring the parental obligation to nurture and guide our children (hopefully, with the help of integrity-centered behaviors) is addressed in the following exchange.

Dear Jim:

As parents of two pre-teens, my husband and I are concerned with some negative trends in our community. These days there is far too much focus on accumulating wealth and the seemingly mindless acquisition of things. We each work and have been able to do pretty well financially. We spend lots of time with our son and daughter and have become concerned that many of their friends, and several of our peers, seem to be caught up in the rush to show how many new things they can own. New cars, clothes, furniture, vacations—well, it is becoming overwhelming. As a couple, we are asking if our own integrity is under siege.

We want to be like others, yet we feel increasingly pressured to go to fashionable places that others like and buy items that commercials promote as essential. We are seeing in our children a gradual tendency to take just about everything for granted.

Have we compromised our values? Have we lost our integrity? We remember that money is the root of all evil and we are feeling guilty. What should we do to re-establish integrity in our lives?

Response:

First of all, money is not the root of all evil; but the love of money is the root of an awful lot of evil. A long time ago, a friend reminded me that we can spend years working to own things that end up owning us. His counsel was to be careful and avoid being controlled by the items we have purchased.

Wealth is not defined by how much individuals have, but how little they need.

Only you can be certain if you have compromised your values or lost your integrity. However, you may find a definition of integrity helpful in establishing a baseline in establishing appropriate principles and behaviors for the future.

Integrity is congruence between what you say and what you do, as well as what you say about what you did. Parents are responsible for setting the ground rules and behaving appropriately. Parents make mistakes and need to own up to their shortcomings immediately. Children learn the real values of the family by observing what their parents do even more than by listening to what parents say.

Integrity is the keystone of leadership, a critical aspect of parenting. The keystone of values holds the family together at its most critical junction, where behaviors are passed along to the next generation. Integrity enables the family to achieve its mission, which sustains civilization. Integrity is the strength, unity, clarity and purpose that upholds and sustains all activities. Integrity provides this stabilizing dimension by never, ever, compromising. Integrity recognizes risks and assumes responsibility. Parents exude integrity and must be willing to push back against the superficial and destructive trends that threaten civility and graciousness.

Now is not the time to lose one's parental nerve. The next generation looks to parental guidance to enable it to safely navigate the turbulent times that are a natural part of moving toward adulthood.

What might you do to re-establish integrity in your lives?

1. Take an inventory of what you own

2. Create a second inventory of what owns you

3. Demonstrate to your children what true appreciation for material and spiritual things means

4. Outline with your teens what legacy you want to leave them

   a. Money

   b. Property

   c. Spiritual principles

   d. Work ethic

   e. Social and cultural tolerance

   f. Any variety of values and behaviors

5. Manage schedules with one another to ensure your legacy

The keystone that sustains an archway is similar to the canopy of love and nurture that caring parents provide a family. The work of the archway's keystone is constant and may go unnoticed until it disappears or collapses. If those keystone values and strengths are not passed along, the family crumbles. Integrity does matter, most especially with the family—the cornerstone of civilization. Don't simply tell them how important values are, show them—soon.

Economic enterprises are engaged in many relationships that have aspects similar to those of a family. Among these are the relationships with the stakeholders, which include the board of directors, employees, investors, educational institutions, customers and even local, state and federal governments. Suppliers (including utility companies, the postal service, providers of raw materials and packaging, etc.) are also partners in economic enterprises. In order to continue their existence, organizations need the products and/or services of their suppliers. Suppliers honor the partnership obligation to meet the organization's needs for an agreed-upon rate of compensation. Conversely, organizations honor the partnership by fulfilling their suppliers' expectations (e.g., providing clear instructions, paying invoices on time and supplying feedback). Within an economic enterprise, the employees are the daily partners working shoulder-to-shoulder to help a leadership team achieve organizational objectives.

If the imagination of employees can be captured by the vision, mission and values of an organization, these stakeholders are likely to be more engaged in a partnership that achieves its goals. There is an energy potential in each of us that is brought into play when we are excited about—and believe in—what we are doing. This energy supplement is not present when we are doing our work simply because we are paid for it, or are compelled by other means.

On behalf of their organizations, integrity-centered leaders communicate the vision ("Where the institution is going"), the mission ("What needs to be accomplished") and the values ("What behaviors are appropriate"). Leaders provide continuing focus on operational priorities, while they direct the organization in its activities. Leaders model appropriate behaviors that inspire the best efforts of their fellow stakeholders. In this process, leaders enable followers to capitalize upon that energy potential. Consistency is a vital element of leadership. With confidence in their leaders, followers know where "true north" is. The integrity of the leader is essential. Another key element is having a longer view that recognizes the need of workers to achieve balance between personal and business priorities in order to bring their best energy to the mission of the organization. As a consequence, thoughtful observers see that integrity is the keystone of leadership. Using this perspective, consider again the wisdom of M.H. McKee: "Integrity is one of several paths; it distinguishes itself from the others because it is the right path and the only one upon which you will never get lost."

Partners with integrity honor obligations. Products and services are delivered as agreed. Suppliers receive clear instructions and are paid on time. Mutual respect can be observed in the gracious behaviors between and among all participants. The following inquiry from an "Integrity Matters" reader helps to illustrate this point.

> Dear Jim:
>
> Last month a substantial number of my clients didn't pay their bills on time. Quite a few do so on a regular basis; they must think it's all right to let it ride as they see fit. I can't afford to cut them loose, and I can't afford to be "the bank," either. How can I guide my clients toward acting with more integrity in their financial transactions with my company?

Response:

> When customers/clients pay late, you may want to assess the situation utilizing these assumptions:
>
> *Assuming* that you are providing excellent services/products and your customers are confirming their satisfaction with all aspects of what you are delivering to them (high quality, superior price-value, along with mutual respect and appreciation),
>
> *Assuming* that you wish to continue working with those "late paying" clients if they would pay as agreed,

Assuming you are willing to risk losing any or all of them if they continue to treat you poorly by failure to meet their part of the agreement (i.e., to pay you on time),

Assuming that you can speak forthrightly to those individuals for whom and with whom you have been providing services,

Assuming that they will respect legitimate concerns that you would share with them related to the difficulties their tardy payments are causing you,

Then consider the following actions:

1. Set a time to meet with each troublesome client face-to-face to confirm your understanding of their thinking regarding not paying you on time.

2. Consider asking each "late-payer" if there is any aspect of your working relationship that is not meeting or exceeding their expectations.

3. Tell them you are beginning to feel that, despite your efforts to deliver to them the very best you could, they must be dissatisfied with some or all of your work or have lost respect for you and/or your services.

4. Explain that you cannot survive long in business if you fail to receive payment from customers, as agreed, for your delivery of goods and services to them.

5. Confirm that you would like to retain your working relationship with them but can only proceed if the integrity of the relationship goes both ways: timely and quality services are followed with timely payments.

Remember: Integrity is the glue of society. Integrity sustains relationships with mutual respect and treats each member of the transaction, whether personally or professionally, as a partner. Partnerships apply to each and every significant relationship.

Finally, if clients do not meet their agreements, and thereby respect high-quality suppliers, bid them farewell. The time you spend on bad-faith clients could have been spent developing and working with new clients who will pay on time.

Interestingly, the above exchange generated the following letter (which was sent to the newspaper that publishes the column) about integrity in relationships.:

I would like to express my appreciation for Jim Bracher's "Integrity Matters" column, to give your newspaper credit for having the backbone to publish it, and to relate two distinct ways it has made a difference in my business and personal life.

First, the column about a receivables problem was right on the mark. I have that in a prominent place on my desk, and I have already referred to it as a blueprint for handling this type of customer issue. Raising a client's awareness in the manner Mr. Bracher suggests has already resulted in better response from, and ultimately better relationships with, my customers.

Secondly, on a more personal note, I am pelted with sales calls on a daily (and nightly) basis. Based on a shifted focus toward integrity (due in no small part to reading Mr. Bracher's column), I asked a long-distance rep if she could fax me a list of social causes her company contributes to. She hung up on me. The response was proof enough that my question was the right one to determine what kind of company I was dealing with.

To close, thank you again for helping to remind us all that there are deeper, more meaningful values by which we may live and work.

As previously mentioned, there are numerous types of partnerships that are attached to any organization, regardless of whether it is a for-profit or a not-for-profit entity. Other stakeholders are also correctly considered partners. Boards of directors engage in performance partnership with the senior leadership, the investing public and the government oversight authorities. Their responsibilities and conduct have been under closer scrutiny during 2003 due to public company scandals; this situation gave an "Integrity Matters" reader the opportunity to pose an interesting set of questions regarding board members.

Dear Jim:

I read a national news front-page article today, Friday, February 21, 2003, regarding a Topeka, Kansas, energy company. A small part of that article discussed the resignation of a board member because of being kept in the dark regarding overcompensation of the CEO. The article also reports the former CEO as saying the board member was simply a poor performer. Two questions arise in my mind.

First, is it not the board's prerogative and responsibility to set the compensation of the CEO in the first place?

Second, assuming the board member indeed was performing poorly, is there not an ethical, moral and perhaps a legal responsibility for board members to take their position seriously and to perform to the best of their ability?

Response:

Yes and Yes to questions one and two.

Number One, boards are responsible for the compensation of the Chief Executive Officer, the boss.

Number Two, board members have financial and legal duties to the stockholders of the company to take their fiduciary responsibilities seriously and perform to the best of their abilities.

Fortunately, the majority of members of boards must be living up to these responsibilities or even more corporate scandals would be wallpapered across the headlines. You can safely assume that most people intend to do a good job.

However, we are uncovering a level of casualness, some might say callousness, regarding the way too many individuals are behaving in positions of responsibility. Sadly for our economy, and our nation, stories of irresponsible leadership at the top, including the board level, bubble onto headlines at an alarming rate.

To underscore your concern, let me repeat a story that was related to me within the last week. A high technology company was holding a board meeting, with several board members participating via telephone. Not very long into the proceedings, a loud swishing sound was heard, above the usual hum of multiple phone connections. As the meeting continued, one officer from the company asked the person phoning in from Colorado if he was on the ski slopes. The board member responded that he was actually skiing down the mountain, but had no idea that the others could hear the noise of the wind, the skis and the snow. The person who told me of the incident was a co-founder of the company. He was dumbfounded, angry and disappointed.

Simply put, how can an individual be giving 100 percent attention to board responsibilities while playing in the snow? Hopefully, this is the exception and not the rule.

Unfortunately, the acquisition of wealth can cause some people to believe that their genius in guiding previous success stories (whether through skill, timing, a strong market or simple luck) makes them immune to the disciplines of listening and focus. Such behavior sets a poor example for those who are charged with daily operations and it is a violation of trust between and among stakeholders (customers, employees, suppliers, investors, etc).

Leadership is about integrity. It never runs away from responsibility.

If you have stock in this company, you have to believe that integrity-centered leadership prevails.

The relationship between a company leadership team and its board of directors is a good example of a multi-level partnership, of interdependence. The leadership team reports to the board, and the board depends upon the information provided to it by the leadership team in order to shape its guidance and counsel. An additional partnership exists between the investing public as well as the overseeing government authorities. Investors, large and small, have every right to expect to be represented by insightful overseers who will protect their economic interests. All of these relationships hang on the integrity of the parties involved, and the outcome of a perceived violation can be serious. In a recent case that was unresolved as of the printing of this book, a high-profile business-woman, the focus of an insider trading investigation, submitted her resignation to the board of the company created by her own initiative and dependent to a degree, still, on her name recognition. This individual appeared to exhibit partnership in submitting her resignation for the good of the institution.

Sometimes boards of directors have no choice but to accept resignations, given their fiduciary responsibilities and the fact that a legal case could take months, perhaps years (given the appeals processes), to wind its way finally through the courts. The stockholders, in partnership with the board, cannot afford to let speculation diminish and perhaps destroy stockholder value.

Another partnership that has a long-term effect on stakeholder value is the relationship of business enterprises to the education system, from which the student can become the source of the raw material that provides intellectual capital. The relationship between economic organizations and the education system is a particularly complex one. It provides an intersection for both government and private funding of research and scholarship, with the sometimes counteracting forces of student and educator ideas, priorities and perspectives. The business enterprise may need engineering talent with practical problem-solving expertise, while the university may be intent on bringing the "just society" of Plato among the liberal arts into the engineering curricula. That this partnership is complex can be seen from the vantage point of a question from an "Integrity Matters" reader regarding the topic of the restoration of trust (in this instance, for academia).

Dear Jim:

I am a 52-year-old president of a pretty successful young semiconductor company. Of the 20 companies the venture capital group who funded us has helped to launch, ours is currently the most successful. We have an industry-wide reputation for excellent product and service quality; five quarters of strong profitability; good prospects for the future; employee and customer loyalty; and, an experienced and professional management team. We are doing well.

Here is my problem: Recently, with 19 other colleagues, each a president of a company in this venture capital firm's portfolio, we were invited to attend a conference where each of us was asked to mention the key attribute for building a successful company. Perhaps it was because I was the oldest executive at the meeting, for my opinion was the first one requested to start the conversation. Without hesitation, I nominated my number one leadership success attribute: Integrity. Can you imagine my shock when more than half of my peers, mostly in their mid to late 30's, laughed aloud? A few others snickered. And the group rushed to replace my word choice of "integrity" and fill the unsettling silence with other terms like "intensity," "competitiveness," "long hours," "intellect," "power network" and "a respected MBA."

What is wrong when this type of thinking becomes the norm? Don't people care about integrity?

Response:

Everything is wrong when those with power, who are also in authority, refuse to respect the human equation in success of any kind. Too many people with executive titles admire rude, calculating and self-serving behavior. Unfortunately, your experience with certain of your colleagues is not unique to business and management. Fortunately, ruthlessness is not yet the norm; but it is gaining on decency. Even so, a significant number of people still care about integrity.

Just a few weeks ago, the sports news told of a recent high school graduate being drafted into the National Basketball Association. Instead of paying tribute to his coaches, who helped him refine his skills over the years, he thanked himself. Rather than offer any appreciation for family and friends who may have gone the extra mile for this gifted young man, he congratulated himself. This is the behavior of someone who believes he is truly self-made. "Immature," "shortsighted" and "selfish" are terms that come to mind. Another description of this style is "arrogant." Unfortunately, this self-centered behavior often continues into adulthood. Sometimes selfishness is obvious in the greed of those gaining wealth and power, made even more obvious by their cruel and vicious comments to those whose values differ from their own. Other times, self-serving behaviors can be seen in temper tantrums by "adults" behaving like overindulged children.

Have you ever played golf with a club thrower? They hit a shot that disappoints them and they let fly; sometimes with brutal language, and at other times with a club. They have allowed their emotions to get the better of them. They fly off the handle. For those who have taken golf lessons, they know that it can be very difficult to predict where a golf club will land once it has been tossed. Controlling a club toss would be made even more unpredictable were the individual upset. I happen to know that club throwing, of any kind, is a dangerous luxury.

At age 15, living in Macon, Missouri, one of my favorite summertime activities was playing croquet. I loved to practice rolling the ball across the lawn and making an excellent cross-court shot. One warm August afternoon, alone at practice, a neighborhood dog chose "my croquet court" for his afternoon break. In times past, cleaning up after the animal was not so serious, a minor intrusion on practice time; however, dusk only allowed a few more rounds and I was not willing to allow the dog his space. So, unsuccessful in chasing the dog away with a yell, I tossed the wooden croquet mallet in the general direction of the invader.

Unbelievably, the handle of the mallet hit the ground and catapulted 30 feet sideways, stunning our neighbor's family pet. Being 30 feet off line is no surprise to me, especially when I recall some of my golf shots these days. Shocked and panicked, I ran to the animal, carried him to the neighbor's front door and explained in tearful apology what happened to their dog, and accompanied them to the veterinarian. Then came the long walk home; where, my parents had been horrified and embarrassed observers. Suffice it to say, I was grounded, with no croquet for quite a while. But, the lesson about self-control has never left me. It is not the right thing to do.

Sometimes damaging behavior is obvious, such as when we see a golf club or croquet mallet thrown. Other times, we might injure those within earshot with a verbal hand grenade, a yell, a cutting comment or condescending laugh. Immature and cruel behavior rots the roots of confidence so necessary for healthy relationships and for those building integrity-centered enterprises.

So, think before acting, verbally and non-verbally. These are tough times for many people. So, listen carefully and caringly to others before reacting and minimize premature and immature responses. Don't carelessly throw a condemning word at a well-meaning colleague.

Please remember: Integrity is the keystone of leadership. It is reflected in discussions, decisions, directives and diagnostics. Leadership emerges from listening, demonstrates character in behavior, and leverages energy with integrity. Integrity is the stabilizing factor that sustains effort and causes energy to create the canopy for accomplishment. Integrity enables the achievement of Vision. Because integrity matters, lend support and add strength to those building for the future.

Nearly all partnerships exist within some type of community. A leader with integrity is aware of this and pays attention to those partnerships that his or her organization has with the community in which it exists. Sometimes this community is expressed in the form of a voluntary association; sometimes it is expressed in the form of a statutory entity (i.e., a government). Multiple partnership interests can be involved.

The introduction of third-party payment via insurance carriers is one of the more complex of all partnerships because of the way it diffuses the chain of responsibility, benefit and reward. The professional is responsible to provide service to the client; the insurance company is responsible to pay the professional for that service. Yet only the client knows whether the service was provided appropriately. The benefit to the professional is provided by the insurance company, who received nothing from the professional (aside from the completed claim). It is not surprising that this arena is the object of governmental regulation and association monitoring on the subject of professional ethics.

An "Integrity Matters" reader expressed a concern that involves the individual professional in partnership with professional associations, with clients, with the clients' insurance carrier, and with the government (through oversight and regulatory impact).

Dear Jim:

I am a professional in a specialty that is carefully monitored by a State Board of Licensure. I am bound by the ethical rules of confidentiality and operate as a private practitioner, educator to licensed professionals, and supervisor of internships for the State Board of

Licensure. Recent demands from health insurance organizations now put my colleagues and myself at ethical risk re: client confidentiality. While we understand that our clients want to use insurance for health-related service, we find ourselves in the untenable position of feeling "bullied" by managed care to breach ethics and give access to confidential information. Even as we discover the risk and terminate agreements to accept certain insurances, we are facing demands to allow managed care staff access to records for past services to their insured.

How can we behave with integrity, protect our client's confidentiality and answer the demands of an entity that asks us to breach ethics that are already monitored by our State Licensing Board?

Response:

Your concerns about integrity cross multiple boundaries and must be addressed one issue at a time.

1. Ethical issues: Once an informed patient asks the counselor/doctor to release information to insurers, the ethics issue disappears. When an informed patient signs a form authorizing the counselor/doctor to furnish information to insurers, this signals to the doctor/counselor that the patient has chosen to utilize funds from a third party (insurance). Then the counselor functions with a lowered obligation of privacy-confidentiality, and the insurer is now able to be involved in the case. This is called informed consent and is both ethical and legal. In this way insurers can protect themselves against those who would abuse the system. It does, however, open the door to some potential for abuse of information.

2. Legal concerns: It is likely that you and your colleagues belong to a professional association that exists, in part, to strengthen your profession, protect your rights and maintain the integrity of those who are licensed colleagues. Quite likely the executive in charge of this association has access to attorneys who can assist in defining needs and creating recommendations to address concerns regarding conflicts of interest and compromising situations. Seek advice and provide input, lest those who are paid to represent you miss the message. It seems that unless you are able to function (consistent with your ethical priorities), your productivity and high-quality service will decline, along with adequate income to support the professional association founded to assist you in the carrying out of your professional expertise. After all, it is from successful members of your profession that your association is funded.

3. Financial implications: Obviously, you must understand all of the requirements of your state's certification procedures as well as the code of ethics of your profession or you could lose your privileges to practice in your chosen profession. Loss of certification has enormous financial ramifications. Morally, legally and financially, you would be wise to know, in detail, from whatever organization is responsible for professional ethics, the best approach that enables you to remain in compliance with any and all professional obligations.

Summary thoughts and suggestions: First, unless or until these issues are resolved, the only way for you to guarantee strict confidentiality is for the client to pay for your services without the benefit of third-party insurance. Those who can afford this may choose this rather than enable an insurer to know their particular problems. This seems, unfortunately, to push hard up against the concept of equal rights to privacy for everyone. Second, your ability to remain effective with the practice you have developed (and at which you hope to continue to earn a good living) depends upon your success in securing legal protection, whether from your association, your state licensing entity or the legislature of your state.

Actions you may choose to take as a concerned licensed service provider, seeking to strengthen your profession:

A. Clarify your ethical concerns with the State Board of Licensure (your professional association can help).

B. Know your rights and responsibilities regarding confidentiality (your attorney and/or your association's attorney can be of immense help in these areas).

C. Define your principles regarding the ethical execution of your duties and measure them against what is currently provided for those in your profession. Where there are differences, you have choices: Create regulations that cause the principles to match or choose to modify your behaviors to live with the existing operating principles. If these options are not adequate, you can always select a new way to make a living.

Remember, each and every one of your patients will understand that integrity is congruence between what you say and what you do, as well as what you say about what you did. Integrity is the keystone of leadership in all fields, including medicine. The keystone holds the profession together at its most critical junction, where knowledge and counsel serve the patient. Integrity is the strength, unity, clarity and purpose that upholds and sustains all of the activities of any medical provider. Leaders in all professions exude integrity.

Integrity-centered leadership is seldom a "sound-bite"-friendly environment. Relationships and obligations demand give-and-take in ways that can appear counterproductive. Patience for mistakes and misunderstandings can appear to be in conflict with bottom-line results and short-term achievements. However, sustaining high performance alongside quality interactions may require flexibility and tolerance. Sometimes what might appear as carelessness can actually be caring, thoughtful behavior.

Be it in a family, an economic organization, voluntary associations or involvement with government at local, state, regional or national levels, we are all partners in the great experiment of life. The partnerships that strive to maintain integrity-centered behavior must be nurtured to help them to be what they were intended to be, an issue addressed in the following exchange.

> Dear Jim:
>
> Is this an integrity issue? My boss expects me to be on time, every time. She is almost never on time for her meetings with me. My frustration is that when her schedule messes up mine, the people who depend on me to not make them wait; well, they get upset with me. If I say anything about my boss not being respectful of my time and how that causes me to be late and disrespectful to others, then I am being unprofessional and disloyal. I have mentioned to her my commitment to not make others wait. She nods and continues her meeting. Abuse of time is not right. Is this violating integrity? Certainly, time costs money. Wasting other people's time is irresponsible.

Response:

> Many wise leaders believe that working effectively requires relationships built upon respect and trust. Pressure to perform is great enough without adding the stresses related to making others wait simply because time commitments are ignored. Emergencies are understood to be the exception. However, some individuals seem to thrive on their tight and tardy schedules. Flying in at the last minute, scrambling for papers and reports, they destroy whatever order might have been necessary for others to function productively.
>
> To make matters worse, many flagrant violators of time seem oblivious to the pain they cause others. This insensitivity runs head-first into

how partners—whether colleagues or bosses, friends or family members—ought to treat one another to enhance trust, respect and productivity. The snowball rolling down the hill is what happens. By the end of the working day, those affected by the clock-wasters can be demoralized. Their plans for managing their efforts have been interrupted, even destroyed. Expending energies in shuffling and adjusting schedules to accommodate the undisciplined leaders takes a toll.

Is such behavior an integrity issue? Yes. Each partner in a relationship, at work or at home, professional or personal, is obligated to show appreciation for the needs of the other. Wasting time, needlessly, is destructive. Partners cannot plan with confidence how best to use their energies. Subordinates in an organization will not maximize productivity when commitments are missed, especially time commitments. Mutual respect suffers. Attitudes of those whose schedules are torn apart will seldom improve.

So, what can be done? Start and end your own meetings on time. Clarify to those who violate time that you need to know what level of rudeness that they find acceptable. If their definition is different from yours, then you will need to make a decision about the lengths to which you will go to keep the relationship alive (personal or professional). After asking for tardy people to behave differently and finding responses unsatisfactory, you will know what to do. If an individual or an organization does not have pride on the timely fulfillment of all commitments, including time, then partnership is difficult, if not impossible. Respect for time is an integrity matter. Partners honor obligations.

One wise consultant offered counsel with regard to the assessment of the strength of partnerships, whether interpersonal or organizational. He suggested asking the following four questions about each stakeholder:

1. Does each participant understand what skill sets and contributions will be required to make the partnership effective?

2. Do all participants feel valued by, and bring value to, the organization?

3. Is every individual committed to the vision of the partnership?

4. Is everyone signed on to the organization's supported behavior and culture?

When the answers are "yes" to each of these four questions, then issues will not polarize nor destroy the partnership or institution. These thoughts lead to successful performance, which is discussed in the next chapter.

Chapter 9
PERFORMANCE:
Accountability Throughout
the Organization

I feel that the greatest reward for doing is the opportunity to do more.
– Jonas Salk

Everyone performs in one fashion or another. Entertainers perform on stages (and sometimes sidewalks) in cities all over the world. Teachers engage in a performance in their classrooms; lawyers do so in courtrooms. It is human performance toward objectives that helps individuals achieve their life goals, and organizations to fulfill their missions. With regard to performance within the context of integrity-centered leadership, the focus is on performance that exceeds expectations. One who leads must exceed the expectations of his or her followers in order to inspire their performance. We are talking about excellence. Performance excellence requires the courage to stay the course, to do the right thing, and maintain balance when faced with the pressures of expediency, politics or short-term gain. Excellence—and integrity—can give birth to courage, and vice versa.

John F. McDonnell, then the Chief Executive Officer of aircraft manufacturer McDonnell Douglas Corporation, said it well:

> The plain fact of the matter is: We no longer live in a world that tolerates *average* or *mediocre* performance. *World-class* performance is a prerequisite for survival. It is no easy feat to lift performance from merely average to world-class. In order to have any hope of meeting that challenge, it is absolutely necessary to *think in different terms* about all of the problems involved in running large, complex businesses.
>
> It is necessary to think in different terms about who the customers are and how to serve them. It is necessary to think in different terms about relations with suppliers and subcontractors. It is necessary to

think in different terms about the systems and processes used in the performance of work. As a related matter, it is necessary to think in different terms about the nature of the relationship between the company and its employees.

In an increasingly competitive world, companies simply cannot afford to treat their people as lifelong dependents who are *entitled* to high wages and many other benefits. By the same token, neither can companies afford to treat their people as unthinking, interchangeable parts with the production machinery. The winners in international competition will be those companies that do the best job of capturing the energy, commitment and creativity of their people.

Enlisting "the energy, commitment and creativity" of an individual requires a vision that captivates the imagination. It also requires a specific and attainable goal, and the reinforcement that is provided by progress reports along the way. It requires the courage of leaders who follow their convictions. Vision, coupled with commitment and sacrifice, leads to achievement.

It is "vision" for a young person to dream of being a world-class athlete by first qualifying for the high school sports team. It is courage to stay the course, to continually push toward—and exceed—one's own expectations, while others are relaxing and living the easier life.

An Olympic gymnastics champion (a gold medallist in 1984), speaking to a large group of senior executives in 1988 at a conference in the Midwest, offered an illuminating story. Before he spoke he demonstrated his prowess on a mini-gym on the stage—and then gave a brief presentation about the nature of excellence. During the Question and Answer session afterward, one of the executives in attendance asked him, "How did you become an Olympic champion? Do you have unusual coordination or strength?"

The champion responded, "No. My basic physical coordination is average, and my childhood was very normal. The difference is that when I first began to learn the gym exercises, I decided to try to make the gymnastics team, and asked the coach how I could do that. He said to work harder than anyone else. I wasn't sure exactly how to do that, but promised myself that I would practice 15 minutes longer than anyone else in the gym. Every day. I thought that by doing this, I would have a good chance to make the school gymnastics team. Well, I did get selected for that gymnastics team. Then, I continued to practice 15 minutes longer than anyone else all season. Again, every day, every time. I improved, and eventually won a college scholarship in gymnastics. Still, I practiced 15 minutes longer than anyone else, and finally made the Olympic team. So, my answer to your question is, the difference between an average gymnast and an Olympic champion is 15 minutes."

There is no doubt more to his success. But this Olympian had a measurement that enabled him to determine progress, and that measure was, at least in the beginning, 15 minutes. It is possible to know when performance is successful only if we have a measurement. Fortunately, almost everything can be measured. Really, it can. Almost anything can be measured in terms of quantity, quality, cost or time. But even this requires a standard for comparison in order for the measurement to be a meaningful number. The gymnast used the practice time of every other athlete in the gym as his standard, and he then exceeded that. He had his own internal performance appraisal system.

And so it is with organizational and individual work performance. To be effective, an individual worker needs performance standards and an appraisal of performance against that standard, or standards, to provide feedback on his or her progress. The organization needs some type of performance matrix (or scorecard) to identify goals and to judge its progress toward the achievement of those goals.

Someone once said, "If you don't know where you are going, any road will take you there." Employees need a plan of action to give them direction with regard to their performance; they also require feedback to learn about the quality of their efforts. In most organizations this is called a "performance appraisal" or "review." It is certainly necessary in today's legal climate to have documentation of substandard performance if any negative actions are to be taken. An organization also cannot simply record the poor performer, lest it be accused of targeting specific individuals. So, everyone's performance level should be documented; or, no one's efforts should be recorded. Integrity-centered organizations pride themselves in their properly documented performance records.

The first mention of employer performance appraisal is unknown, although it has been the subject of many books and articles. Unfortunately, the emotions connected with performance appraisals have been troublesome ever since the concept was first introduced long ago. Does anyone want to be labeled as anything other than "excellent"? Some employees may feel unfairly judged because of an arbitrary boss. Such performance communication strains are counterproductive.

An integrity-centered performance appraisal process will ensure that boss and employee agree upon the duties and responsibilities; on the conditions that will exist when those have been satisfactorily performed, and review the facts and milestones of performance. Even if employees are in the right organization for their values, challenging situations sometimes arise. Performance appraisal methods can be as controversial as the judgment itself, as noted in the following letter from one of our readers.

Dear Jim:

My company has a performance review policy requiring that an arbitrary percentage of its employees fits into a particular rating category. I received a significantly lower review score than I should have. My manager said that "compared to all others, that's how it works out." This means a much lower bonus and options for next year. Is this fair?

Response:

A long time ago, someone suggested to me that I could exceed an unlimited budget. Once it became clear to me that this was not a compliment, my spending habits changed.

Everyone sees themselves as "above average," and there is a chance your manager has been fair. On the other hand, if you are a high performer and are truly failing to be recognized and rewarded for it, ask your supervisor how to improve your productivity. After all, you want to be in the top group. Once you know what to accomplish, you can then determine if your leader is eager to support your quest for success, or if your leader simply sees you as a statistical contributor who enables others to gain more substantial rewards.

No matter which way things turn out, you will know a lot more about the integrity of your boss and your organization. The answer will determine your tenure.

The integrity of those performing in positions of public trust is an area of special interest with regard to the restoration of confidence. Government officials, whether elected or appointed, must have a special relationship with "the people"; this relationship carries with it an obligation to act in the public's best interest. Often the public's perception of solid performance is as important as the actual execution of duties. This can be illustrated by the behavior of a very young governor of a Midwestern state. Upon arriving in his new office, he found boxes of stationery that were left over from the previous administration. What did he do? He recycled the paper, crossing out the previous governor's name, and had his name typed on the same letterhead. He may have saved only a few thousand dollars by doing this, but he communicated a million dollars worth of concern for the state's budget over his own ego. What were the actions of that young governor worth to the taxpayers of his state?

However, not every public servant performs with such integrity-centered behavior. Special words have been reserved, even invented, to describe ways the public trust may have been violated when officials fail to achieve high levels of performance. These terms include:

> "Nonfeasance"—failing to perform in office, but resulting in no legal liability to the office holder.

> "Misfeasance"—doing the improper or wrong thing, in which some legal repercussions may exist.

> "Malfeasance"—performing an act that is not within the scope of the position; here again, there may be legal ramifications.

These definitions sometimes overlap and require the help of a lawyer to be understood. However, when public service behaviors generate the need to examine performance in this critical detail, then it is time to place the subject of accountability on center stage. Regardless of where one is evaluated on any given review of effectiveness in politics, business or public service, there is always the need to distinguish between form and substance. Responsible citizenship requires maintaining a distinction between what is important—substance—and the things that are simply disliked. It is all too common that friction results from personal likes and dislikes, which can generate emotional heat leading to irrational and destructive behaviors.

Two popular subjects that often generate such friction and heat are politics and religion. Practically everyone has opinions, often strongly held, in both areas. On occasion, offering strongly held opinions outside of one's publicly accepted field of expertise can elicit powerful reactions. For example, it is no surprise when fireworks erupt in response to political leaders who make pronouncements about personal lifestyle issues, or when educators feel compelled to provide political commentary.

One of our readers was particularly concerned about the application of these concepts to a situation involving a California university, and presented this issue in the following letter.

> Dear Jim:

> I note with alarm that the Academic Senate of UCLA, which is a tax-supported, public university, has taken it upon itself to pass a resolution to condemn the war in Iraq (now that it is largely over) and place the governing of Iraq in the hands of the United Nations, which has consistently failed to do a competent job with this type of assignment from the

date of its formation. I believe it is unethical for a publicly supported university to politicize its academic role in this manner. Furthermore, faculty members of the Senate who oppose this action of the Senate cannot resign from the Senate without also resigning their jobs as professors at the university—so much for academic freedom! Free speech at UCLA, and possibly other institutions, requires a dissenting professor to commit career suicide! What do you think?

Response:

Academic arrogance and intellectual intolerance seem to have joined arms in the controversy you describe regarding the behavior of certain faculty senate members at UCLA. Academic freedom and respect for the world of ideas seem to be the victims here. The UCLA Faculty Senate's contempt for debate signals the rigidity of closed minds. Refusing to acknowledge the legitimacy of conflicting opinions sets in motion the building of "camps" that are readying for the mindless protection of ideas. Universities were never intended to behave that way. For it is in the free exchange of ideas that new concepts can emerge. Millions of lives have been lost in the protection of these very First Amendment rights.

With reference to academic bodies making pronouncements, well, that deserves some careful investigation. Unless or until the academic charter of a publicly funded educational institution specifically permits or requires political pronouncements, they seem wholly inappropriate or simply irrelevant.

The interesting dimension of your question about political opinions is that they are quite a bit like religious perspectives. Almost everyone you meet is an expert in each area. ...

... Today, we need our best and brightest university talent to solve real problems like the killer epidemic caused by Severe Acute Respiratory Syndrome or SARS. We need communications expertise that facilitates understanding between and among conflicting multinational cultures, especially as rebuilding is required in nations recently delivered to freedom from tyranny. We need business training programs that prepare leaders to function with a social conscience that is built on an ethical foundation. Shall I go on?

Perhaps these academics feel a need to save society. That may or may not be their expertise. Society might be better served if they would spend their time sharpening their pedagogical skills.

It should be common knowledge that free markets, including academic institutions and their faculty senates, must regulate themselves or governments will.

We know that effectively communicating a sense of urgency, commitment to excellence and the acceptance of accountability must be demonstrated by those who assume leadership roles throughout society. When leaders abdicate, followers can too easily stumble.

Performance accountability of leadership is not limited to elected officials, bureaucrats or corporate leaders. Accountability extends to those who enjoy high visibility and would use their celebrity to influence an adoring public in areas outside of their realm of expertise or talent. Celebrities who take controversial positions sometimes break through the thin ice of popular support. Such was the case with the singing group the Dixie Chicks, about whom an "Integrity Matters" reader asked the following question.

Dear Jim:

The Dixie Chicks, a very popular Country and Western singing group, is catching a large amount of heat for remarks one of the members of the group made in England recently, expressing her embarrassment over the policies and the leadership of President Bush with reference to the war in Iraq. The group has not really apologized for those remarks and now the group is posing nude in the May 4 *Entertainment Weekly* magazine.

Are they exhibiting integrity? As a former enthusiastic Dixie Chicks fan, I am upset and wonder if it is their lack of ethics regarding patriotism or simply greed that drives them. They are different now and I am not happy. What have I missed?

Response:

The Dixie Chicks have every right to express their ideas, anywhere and anytime, and on any topic. Fans have a right to expect consistency and predictability from their entertainers. When these freedoms (for the entertainers) and the expectations (from the fans) get too far apart, the relationship can deteriorate. When relationships between stars and fans break, then the business success of the entertainers will often move in a downward spiral. Please be assured, the Dixie Chicks are not unique in disappointing fans.

About 35 years ago, one member of a famous music group at that time, the Beatles, announced while traveling outside Europe and America that he felt that his singing group was having a greater impact on the world than had Jesus, the source of faith and inspiration for those who follow the Christian faith. These four young men from Liverpool, England, created a firestorm that lasted a while. They gained and lost fans, in large numbers. Some Beatle fans expressed outrage and felt they had been let down.

Today, the Dixie Chicks, three talented singers-songwriters-performers, have built a fabulously successful reputation that has suddenly changed, at least in your eyes. They had become famous providing a certain kind of entertainment that included not only their brand of music, but also a predictable public image. For whatever reasons, much about them seems to have flip-flopped in how you see the Dixie Chicks and how they are presenting themselves to the public.

In clear business terms, they have a right to offer any product and image they choose. You can elect to accept or reject their new package. In your eyes they have violated a trust and their decisions to pose nude are a radical departure of the brand image you had expected from them. The actions being taken by the Dixie Chicks may not violate our definition of integrity. They seem to be choosing activities (controversial political positions and crass nudity for the marketing of some changing professional image) that seem to be far different from what you and others had come to expect from them. These are their choices.

However, when public figures attract a great deal of attention, often associated with money, influence and celebrity, there may be unspoken requirements that activities that detract from the accepted image are not acceptable. Like it or not, we look to these leaders (entertainment, sports, government, religion, education, military, media, medicine and a whole host of other admirable roles within society) and we need for them to provide steadiness in an uncertain world.

The Dixie Chicks' current crisis is a good reminder for everyone. In one way or another, who among us is not responsible as a role model for someone? What the Dixie Chicks can teach us is that there are consequences when we choose not to control our behaviors, public or private. Those who look to leaders know that integrity matters and a predictable model of behavior can be a source of strength for those about us.

Each of us has developed an image or a brand that others around us have come to appreciate, expect, and, upon which they are comfortable turning to when they make decisions. Parents and teachers, physicians and attorneys, elected officials and business executives, brothers and sisters, religious leaders and media moguls—each can improve society and enhance individual and organizational effectiveness when the brand or image represented to those who need them most is taken seriously.

Take your own inventory of who you are and what others need from you, and be honest:

1. What brand or image do you create or represent for:
   friends and acquaintances?
   family members, direct and extended?
   spouse-partner?
   children and grandchildren?
   business associates?
   customers?
   suppliers?
   voters?
   fellow travelers?
   every conceivable encounter of life?

2. Are you conscious of any limitations created by your image or brand?
   dress code?
   language (grammar, topics, vulgarity)?
   treatment of others?
   acceptance of responsibility when things go poorly?
   passing out compliments when things go well?

3. What are you doing to strengthen your legitimate reputation?

4. What are the consequences for you, your impact and your success if you ignore the roles and responsibilities (image and brand) others have come to expect from you?

Your question about a successful music group's new and changing behavior is a loud signal for many individuals to carefully assess how seriously they look at who they are in the eyes of those with whom they relate every day. There are consequences when we ignore the needs of those about us. The Dixie Chicks worked long and hard to build a large and loyal fan base who cared for their special brand of entertainment.

A reputation takes years to build and can be destroyed in a minute. The same applies to every reader of the column. Integrity matters in each and every transaction and relationship. Think before you speak. Think twice before you act.

Responsible execution of duties is required both personally and organizationally. The furor over the compensation of the former chairman of the New York Stock Exchange in 2003 was not directed at the success of his work. Wall Street and Main Street were up in arms about the perceived greed and selfishness of a gigantic pay package. Although the heat was directed at Richard Grasso, there may come a time when the board members will need to answer questions about their own decision to sanction such payments. This situation is about leadership—all the way to the organization's board of directors. In fact, Grasso's performance was never the issue. However, the performance of the board was an issue—and remains so. This compensation crisis generated the following letter to the "Integrity Matters" column.

Dear Jim:

The board of the New York Stock Exchange decided to pay its top administrator a gigantic amount of money. Perhaps you will comment on the $140 million accumulated back pay and benefits paid to Richard Grasso, chairman and chief executive. Who will pay for these obscene fees? It is the little people, yet again.

Response:

Chairman Richard Grasso's acceptance of the $139.5 million has reignited the debate over standards of governance at the world's largest stock exchange. His package is greater than the NYSE's total net income for the past three years. Though perfectly legal, the huge payout feeds the public's perception of Wall Street as a rigged game that enriches a few big players, while small investors get bilked.

Who is responsible for this gigantic compensation? It's the Board of Directors of the New York Stock Exchange. The board appears to have acted very generously, possibly irresponsibly, certainly insensitively. For starters those rewarding Grasso (the compensation committee and board) are individuals and organizations over whom he has regulatory authority and responsibility. This has some parallel to a group of motorists directly rewarding the police officer who has the authority to enforce traffic laws.

Where the money is coming from might become clearer when we know that a group of 1,366 seat-holders of the NYSE is planning a lawsuit to force Grasso to renegotiate his controversial pay package. If they feel "on the hook" for Grasso's windfall, then some of their customers—e.g., individual investors—may feel the sting of costs that can be legally passed along.

Here is what we do know: Free markets must regulate themselves or governments will. It does not take a rocket scientist to recognize that oversight committees and other similarly chartered organizations have a responsibility to protect themselves and the public from both real and perceived of conflicts of interest. Whether Grasso is overpaid is not the concern of this column. However, the appearance of becoming compromised in the pursuit of oversight harms the enterprise and can demoralize an investing public already discouraged by the bombardment of news that continues reporting scandalous behaviors throughout our society.

By way of summary, here are some of the integrity-related leadership issues:

Grasso's first duty is to set a good example. His pay package does anything but. It serves as a tacit endorsement of NYSE companies that have paid executives lavishly while their firms have languished. His acceptance of a big payment financed by the companies he regulates creates the appearance of a conflict of interest.

Worst of all, though, Grasso's pay undermines the NYSE's own efforts to promote corporate reform. It has offered a number of proposals to encourage corporate boards to stand up to their CEOs and hold top executives more accountable. Yet the nine-figure compensation suggests a board only too eager to please its own chairman.

Greed is hardly new or surprising. But its display by a public watchdog such as the New York Stock Exchange suggests Wall Street may still have a long way to go to clean up its act. When leaders ignore the importance of maintaining a proper balance between self-interest and social responsibility, the free market is at risk.

Subsequent to the above exchange, Grasso reportedly gave up another $48 million in future compensation in an effort to satisfy critics. Despite this action, cries for his resignation grew from the members of the NYSE as well as the pension fund community, which relies upon the trust of the integrity of the NYSE Board and leadership. These cries reached a crescendo on September 17, 2003;

Grasso resigned his position that afternoon. The New York Stock Exchange Board of Directors and its Compensation Committee continue under the pressure of public scrutiny, and we can hope that these individuals will remodel the structure of their governance to remove even the appearance of a conflict of interest in their performance.

Integrity-centered leaders expect the spotlight to be shining on them 24 hours a day, 7 days a week. How individuals behave determines the long-term viability of their effectiveness. Trust is an integral part of any performance equation. When laws are broken, credibility suffers. At no time in recent history has there been a greater need to restore confidence in a "level playing field."

The current investigation of Olympic and professional athletes suspected of using performance-enhancing drugs is another reminder of the challenges related to maintaining a level playing field. Likewise, those who violate appropriate confidential briefings to win illegal financial rewards highlight the critical need to restore performance integrity in financial markets. This concern was addressed in the following question from an "Integrity Matters" reader.

> Dear Jim:
>
> You are a consultant. What is your response about the level of integrity exhibited by the Wall Street consultant-economist, Peter Davis, who has pleaded guilty to fraud and conspiracy? According to what has been written, he attended confidential Treasury Department news conferences and then rushed, using a cell phone, to notify Goldman Sachs about sensitive, advance information regarding the bond market, where they made $3.8 million in illegal profits. It seems that the extra eight-minute edge on the rest of the market that his information provided to the crooks at Goldman Sachs was enough time to provide this wealthy firm with even more profit-taking opportunities. Is this behavior commonplace on Wall Street? What does this behavior say about consultants?

Response:

> Integrity is never for sale. Mr. Peter Davis has admitted that he is guilty of violating trust and cheating. He deserves to suffer the consequences of his actions. However, what about his fellow participants from Goldman Sachs? They accepted illegal insider information. How disappointing for the financial industry and our society. This particular incident comes on the heels of the board of directors of the New York Stock Exchange approving a $139.5 million controversial pay package for its

chief executive, Mr. Richard Grasso. Neither of these events will help restore confidence in the leadership of our nation's investment community. Without a balance between self-interest and social responsibility, greed displaces responsible leadership behavior.

Honest individuals, in any walk of life, including consultants like me, are diminished by the destructive and selfish behaviors of those who work in their field of endeavor. A colleague who violates accepted standards of conduct infects reputation and stature, sometimes a little and at other times, very seriously. Corruption and misbehavior, whether illegal or simply inappropriate, erode confidence and trust between and among members of a community — whether small or large, business or social, political or religious. What each person says and does really matters.

The good news, according to a report from the Associated Press, about this situation is that the United States Attorney, Mr. James Comey, has said, "A scheme to steal confidential information from the Treasury Department and tip off others shakes the confidence of the investing public and it is not to be tolerated." Mr. Davis violated the embargo, meaning that he was obligated not to disclose any information ahead of time.

The proof of Mr. Comey's comments regarding not tolerating such behavior will become real when those who were involved with Mr. Davis, from Goldman Sachs, are identified and dealt with effectively. Until this type of behavior is rooted out and all participants are brought to justice, the word "scapegoat" is not far below the surface. Controlling greed and selfishness is essential in order for our culture to be sustained. Democracy and free market capitalism depend upon the constancy of integrity—throughout the system. Integrity is the keystone for sustaining our social, economic and cultural structure.

The performance question to be answered for any organization is this: When individuals (including senior executives) violate trust, do not honor commitments, or fail to meet quality standards, are they given due process and then, if necessary, replaced? For an integrity-centered organization, the answer must reflect the confidence of every stakeholder that accountability reaches from the front-line employee to the organization's very board members themselves.

Chapter 10

CHARITY:
Generous Community Stewardship

*The most terrible poverty is loneliness
and the feeling of being unwanted.
– Mother Teresa*

*Unreal is action without discipline;
charity without sympathy; ritual without devotion
– Bhagavadgita*

As an attribute of integrity, "charity" refers to the broad view that we should
be alert to the opportunity to serve the less fortunate, and do so by giving of our
time and our resources. It is useful to remember that the environment cannot tell
us what it needs; animals are unable to express their needs; and not all people are
able or willing to articulate their needs. We can therefore speak of charity as an
organization dedicated to assisting those in need of help. We can speak of individuals with integrity behaving with generosity and assisting others. Finally, we
can speak of an organization having a charitable orientation within its culture. In
each instance, charity has a great deal to do with being attentive to others. Charity is the generosity of consistently giving back to the community.

Religious organizations have built powerful and positive reputations channel-
ing a great deal of money and energy to serve those who need assistance. For thousands of years, on behalf of millions of people, service-oriented institutions have
done "good works." An ordained clergyman of a Midwestern church often reminded parishioners that they were to give, not because they must but because they may.
Generosity serves the giver and recipient best when the gift is offered willingly,
enthusiastically and appreciatively. Certainly, needed dollars can be secured even
from a clenched fist, and that may be necessary at times. Guilt, obligation and

group pressure can be used in order to raise important funds, but over the long haul, the internally driven donor will deliver the highest level of commitment.

One of the greatest charitable acts that an economic organization can provide is to remain healthy, providing jobs for people who might otherwise not have them, as well as supplying the wages, bonuses and perhaps the dividends that help to fuel our free market system. A new company may not yet understand its business cycle well enough to know what it might be able to give away and what amounts to reserve for its future. Further, a business exists in a competitive environment, and monies used in one area may take opportunity away from other parts of the financial equation. In the following letter, an "Integrity Matters" reader posed a question relating to just this issue.

> Dear Jim:
>
> As a local business owner, I have always felt that I have run my business the "right way." I have kept my word to my customers, employees and vendors; I have trained my staff well; and I have rewarded and advised my people irrespective of gender or ethnicity. I have followed your columns each Wednesday and, for the most part, have agreed with your advice. Overall, I think you are helping people on either the customer or employer side of the business equation. You are able to clearly distinguish acceptable from unacceptable behavior. However, I took exception to a recent column of yours in which you seemed to suggest that you could apply eight attributes to a business relating to its integrity and that if it failed of any of the attributes, and then it wasn't an ethical company.
>
> I believe you should consider two factors: if a company's right standards put it at a disadvantage to its competitors to the point where it can't survive, then nobody wins. Community involvement you seem to consider as one of the nine criteria for a company to maintain integrity. Yes, I agree, yet it is clear to me that heavy involvement here is a luxury that comes only after profitability and taking care of employees.
>
> I do well in most answers to your integrity questions, but not all. It seems to me that you are suggesting that an individual not be satisfied with a company unless they have got the right answer to the each and every one of your "integrity test" questions.
>
> Can you cut me a little slack here? I've actually urged many members of my staff here to read your column. Now that they've seen your yardstick for being a truly ethical company, I'm starting to hear some

grumbling. I don't want to feel sorry I recommended your "Integrity Matters" column, but we have some people who were quite content with their company (my company) who now aren't so sure.

Now, what do I do?

Response:

From the way you describe your business and your leadership, you have every right to be proud of your own high-principled operation as well as the effectiveness of your company.

Regarding answering affirmatively regarding all eight attributes of integrity and leadership, please understand that these are guidelines and not hard and fast rules. When the "Integrity Matters" column was asked to establish criteria for identifying high-integrity organizations, our questions became the starting point.

When a leader or an organization falls short in any or several of the suggested nine areas, then there could be opportunities for growth and engagement. Growth opportunities (sometimes disguised as challenges) seem to emerge often for leaders to showcase their desire to listen and improve. When employees, customers and suppliers see an organization trying to improve (and improving), their levels of confidence are likely to improve. Engagement with various stakeholders to help a responsive leader to find ways to improve (in any or all of the nine areas) brings a new and healthy partnership for the enterprise. Every participant has ownership in the progress of the institution, company or department. Asking for help is a sign of openness and willingness to get stronger. So, go ahead and ask for help.

Your reference to "grumbling" is probably another good sign. Your people are communicating that they do expect more from you and your organization. Obviously, they believe you are not only willing to listen, but also you are capable of doing something about making improvements. Acknowledge all of this wonderful "grumbling" as a call for action and prove how right your people are to believe in you.

You mentioned that community involvement is more of the luxury of the already successful. Not necessarily! Some companies decide early on to "reach out" in small ways to demonstrate their social commitment in those communities where they conduct business. In the early (often struggling) days, "sweat" and time are what is contributed. This behavior announces to all who are affected that leadership really cares.

When leaders wait until such commitment is convenient and comfortable, it may be too late to teach (by example) that sacrifice is a part of the soul of an integrity-centered organization. The sooner you set the tone, the sooner you reap the rewards of commitment and involvement—both for and with your people, your community and your own business enterprise.

Leadership allows people the chance to develop a community-stewardship culture in their organizations. Giving back to the community in return for the opportunity to succeed is the obligation of the socially responsible, and is an indicator of integrity. We can help the community in whatever ways are possible for us, and which may not involve financial risk; this is the larger concept of charity. Embracing this larger concept of charity as community involvement was clearly on the mind of another of our readers, who was faced with a conflict between personal values and those of an employer.

Dear Jim:

My boss was approached by the Red Cross to have a blood drive. He refused to participate because he does not want to disrupt one day's work. Now he won't even give us time off to go on our own, using available "personal business time" that is part of our benefit package. What can we do, and what do you think of this?

Response:

First, what do I think? Your boss is making a mistake. Shortsightedness is a luxury our society cannot afford. Your boss is missing an important opportunity to safeguard against emergencies. Regardless of what one chooses to support in areas of charitable giving, refusing to donate blood is risky and foolish. Statistical information underscores the universal need for blood. Emergencies affect a large segment of our population. As our nation continues to become older, it should be obvious that there is a growing need for adequate blood supplies.

Terrorism and those who carry out horrific societal sabotage must be taken seriously. Now, more than ever before, we are required, just as the Scouting Oath demands, to always be prepared. Having enough "clean blood" is imperative. We cannot wait until we are in the middle of events such as floods, fires, tornadoes, hurricanes, plane crashes and other catastrophes to get ready. Keeping the blood bank fully stocked is essential.

My thoughts are quite clear about a boss who is not interested in functioning proactively in areas related to adding to a community's blood supply. My reaction can be remembered with three letters of the alphabet: SOS. This type of thinking is simply Stuck On Shortsightedness! If it were not such a serious lapse in judgment, it might warrant spending energy in teaching the individual about the services of the American Red Cross and its lifesaving contributions. But, from your description of this "production-driving" supervisor, it might be a waste of energy, at least for the present.

However, yours is still the challenge of what to do about the blood drive. Here are some steps to keep the blood reserves strong for your community:

1. Reconnect with the Red Cross and donate your own blood, immediately

2. Encourage your colleagues to do the same

3. Contact the human resources department and learn your company's policy about utilizing personal business time

4. Cut the boss a little slack; assume that he really does support building up blood reserves and that he might have good reasons for not wanting to impact productivity at this time

5. Circle back with the boss, in a less stressful business cycle, and ask when might be the best time of the year for supporting the blood drive, and communicate the better schedule to the Red Cross or an appropriate agency.

When readers pose questions to the "Integrity Matters" column, the full context is almost never known. The boss in the previous example may have had a bad experience in this area, or may indeed lack a charitable nature. Whatever the specifics of that person's character, donating blood demonstrates one of the areas in which a business can behave charitably without risking its ability to be profitable, while providing a forum in which individual employees can also behave charitably. Among any sizeable group of employees, there will be those who are deeply involved in charitable pursuits. Sometimes these efforts are church-related; other times they may be related to areas such as medical research. Some employees will resent overt efforts on the part of people in their workplace to interfere with their own volunteering. Socially engaged employees will appreciate working for an employer who makes these efforts easier, and even more so when efforts to reach out and assist others are directly supported.

Since the first rule of a business is to survive (by staying healthy), a company would not serve the community or its employees if it were to jeopardize its solvency by giving away more money than it could afford. Such behavior might invite justifiable ridicule to the degree that it violates common sense. However, an organization that is not yet profitable can behave charitably by encouraging its employees to behave charitably—by sharing their resources. This idea has given rise to the United Way concept of shared giving. But such collective giving can also generate feelings of coercion, as is described in the following "Integrity Matters" dialogue.

Dear Jim:

The company I work for is actively involved with the United Way. In addition to corporate support, each employee, including myself, is "encouraged" by the chief executive officer to contribute. I would rather contribute to other organizations and not feel as if I "have to" contribute to the United Way. What can I do?

Response:

Because the United Way has created a reputation of good deeds, it is often difficult to "opt out" of the contribution expectations. Given the competitive format (namely, what percentage of employees participate), it may be cumbersome "career-wise" to not contribute.

As with many volunteer efforts, the metrics can sometimes be more admirable than the tactics. Each company wants to demonstrate to their stakeholders high marks trending toward 100 percent charitable participation. This goal is worthy, but not if achieved through pressuring participation.

Ask yourself if the "work" of the United Way is within your personal budget. If yes, participate. If no, then find a way to gain understanding with those directing the efforts, perhaps by showing them the positive contributions you are making to others, or by asking United Way to direct your contributions to a specific recipient.

Sometimes a business will demonstrate charity by giving funds, but for a business-oriented reason. One can argue from a "bottom-line perspective" that the only time a business is justified in giving money to charity is when that donation furthers the welfare of the company itself. For example, when a manager makes a donation from company funds, it might be criticized as an ill-advised expenditure of the owner's (stockholder's) investment unless it furthers the firm's economic interests. For this reason, many companies have established committees to examine proposed donations to ensure that the owner's (stockholder's) interest are protected, and that the donations are evaluated on their reciprocal value to the organization. It is not our place to judge whether this is charity or marketing; what seems to be important here is that all parties are served, legally and morally. Of course, the fact that businesses typically approach charitable giving from the point of view of their own enlightened self-interest provides an opportunity for manipulation, so-called "spin," as one of our readers observed.

> Dear Jim:
>
> When a major public company moved its home office to our city, its leaders immediately made a major donation to save the symphony orchestra. They were lauded by the media, and acquired the reputation of being community-minded. They have done nothing since, and that donation, averaged over the years, renders it small by comparison to other companies like my own that consistently give smaller amounts without fanfare, year after year. Why do those in the leadership of the media not pick up on this? This same large public company still enjoys the highest reputation for philanthropy in the public mind, and it is a sham!

Response:

> Integrity-centered leaders and organizations are not the "flash in the pan" show-boaters. Sustained commitments are the foundation of civilization and society. When the balance is "out of kilter" between self-interest and social responsibility, then all stakeholders suffer. Your description of how an organization comes into your community and receives significant and positive media coverage for their one-time contribution should be embarrassing to those who contribute to perpetuating such a "myth" of sincerity and integrity.
>
> You emphasize your own continuous support of your local community and wonder why the media falls all over itself when a "newcomer" or sudden "big- spending donor" drops a large contribution in a highly visible manner. Why, in contrast, does your charitable steadiness, and the giving of many others like you, seemingly go unnoticed by these same types of news organizations?
>
> The answer could be simple arithmetic. Perhaps those who made the contributions are also excellent prospects for sizable advertising dollars.

Maybe their economics make them more attractive. Or, maybe the splash made by the "newly arrived corporate contributor" was well-orchestrated by their very own community and public relations professionals. And it could be that you are missing something about this organization's charitable behavior, and the way in which it has been covered by the media, in your observations.

Regardless of what is correct or incorrect about your perceptions of the "flash in the pan" situation you describe, this much can be known: Integrity is not a one-time activity. Over and over, integrity-centered leaders and organizations play by the rules, do what is right, support worthy causes, and treat fellow stakeholders as partners and peers. What is known as "integrity-centered" in business always revolves around honesty, consistency and accountability. In fact, there are eight question areas that can help individuals to pinpoint the qualities of an "Integrity-Centered Company":

Eight Question Areas to Build an Integrity-Centered Company

1. CHARACTER: Consistency Between Word and Deed
   Do the leaders of your organization exhibit congruence between what they say and what they do, as well as what they say about what they did?

2. HONESTY: Truthful Communication
   Do you have confidence that your leaders would never engage in or sanction misrepresentation?

3. OPENNESS: Operational Transparency
   Is appropriate information about your organization readily available?

4. AUTHORITY: Employee Encouragement
   Are you able to correct a customer problem? Do you have confidence that your actions will be supported?

5. PARTNERSHIP: Honor Obligations
   Does your organization pride itself on the timely fulfillment of all commitments?

6. PERFORMANCE: Accountability Throughout the Organization
   If individuals, including senior executives, underperform repeatedly, are they given due process and then, if necessary, replaced?

7. CHARITY: Generous Community Stewardship
   Does your organization reach out to those in need?

8. GRACIOUSNESS: Respect and Discipline
   Does your organization demonstrate care and concern for all
   stakeholders?

When you assess the "big-spending sprinter" company that received
the media attention with a one-time splashing gift to the symphony, do
you believe their organizational behaviors reflect the eight principles
outlined above? If "No" is your answer on more than two of the eight,
then you can be confident that some of their core values are not integrity-
centered. Their character, perhaps even the motivation of their leaders,
might be suspect. Certainly, you have not been impressed.

There is a tremendous difference between business "sprinters" and
"marathoners." The sprinters show a burst of enthusiasm and then
after 100 meters or yards, they are fatigued. They gave their all for the
immediate speed that they attained. For the short distance, they are
fast, but their speed won't last. Others, less flashy or fast, demand of
themselves substantial efforts in preparation for the longer-distance
efforts. The 26 miles of running are managed differently and exact a
different toll. Marathoners understand the sacrifice and weather the
grueling fitness schedule. Each of the distances is demanding of its participants. Yet, the integrity-centered leader, the one known for character, is often identified with the distance-demanding requirements. And,
as we have learned, character is the ability to carry out the resolution
long after the initial burst of enthusiasm is gone. Character shows when
decisions are implemented.

Communities depend upon the generosity of the business marathoners. They are the foundation, the superstructure and the operational
strength of most of what is good in our culture. They may never become
the darlings of the media, but they—and those like them—are the soul of
our society.

Charitable organizations have experienced a strengthening partnership with
corporate giving. Public and corporate participation in charitable collection
efforts tends to increase during periods of emergency, and decrease during periods of scandal, such as that which affected the national United Way leadership in
the early 1990's. When donors are concerned about how their money will be
used, they tend to hold on to it. Even when the president of a large corporation

speaks in favor of the worthiness of a charitable agency, he or she can encounter difficulty in overcoming the effects of public scandal. Unfortunately, worthwhile charities that receive funding in this manner can suffer a serious loss of support as a consequence. One of our readers was concerned with exactly this potential effect, described in the following letter.

> Dear Jim,
>
> I am having a problem reconciling what is happening in certain parts of organized religion and the various scandals including the latest pedophilia mess. Here is my dilemma: If I stop giving to my church out of concern that its leaders are using the money irresponsibly and unethically in dealing with these scandals, then what about worthwhile charitable activities helped by my church donations? I am frustrated and concerned and feel this issue is about integrity. What do you think?

Response:

> You have raised an interesting and valuable concern. Integrity is at the heart of the issue. It appears that current administrative costs in some churches are high and that some of these religious institutions and charities have engaged in practices that turn off many people, including you. Some have used donations to make settlements to fight their legal conflicts instead of using the funds for the named purposes of the institution. Their decisions to spend financial resources for one purpose after raising the funds for a very different purpose lack consistency and integrity. Many loyal believers have felt betrayed.
>
> Recently, tens of millions of dollars were earmarked in Massachusetts to pay settlements related to lawsuits directed at ordained priests who abused young people. It is unthinkable that the caring and generous parishioners who donated those millions of dollars intended for their sacrificial giving to pay for legal problems created by such destructive behaviors. If this were a business transaction, it might be called "bait and switch"—the unsuspecting buyer is shown one product, asked to pay for it, only to be provided something very different, worth a great deal less. Such an event in business would be described as fraud, with legal and financial consequences. It is common sense that charitable organizations must operate with the same stringent operational rules as the rest of business and society.
>
> The example to which you refer by your question, namely, that of

pedophilia, has been one of the most disturbing. However, responsible parish councils, pastors and their congregations are working through that known set of problems. It seems probable that the involved religious institutions and other social service organizations will emerge wiser and with new and stronger self-regulating processes. Usually, appropriate solutions emerge after a crisis with both religious institutions and secular charities. It is also true that our society has a network of socially responsive and critical services that are sustained by organized religion. These charities, and many others, do a lot of good for people who might have no other place to turn.

You may, of course, simply move your money to another church or charity. That is quick and direct and has the virtue of removing you from any need to get involved with those who have disappointed you. You need to decide if the greater good is served by cutting off the charities with known, visible problems, and shift the money to charities with which you have less connection, but whose reputations are, for now at least, unblemished.

Another and perhaps more prudent approach might be to get involved directly with the institutions you support; organizations engaged in work relevant to your interests. Your involvement might improve their administrative and professional performance. In this way you can continue to support them so long as they are working through their problems responsibly. The larger safety net provided by your charitable institution is thereby protected and even improved.

If leaders of charities you support remain unresponsive to the need for change, then your issue becomes very clear, and you will very likely move your charitable giving to more responsive providers. How wonderful that people with your values are concerned and involved. Integrity matters.

Charity is considered to be an attribute of integrity-centered individuals and organizations because each individual is made better by giving time, materials, support and funding to those who deserve assistance. Furthermore, the whole of society is strengthened when the leaders of our institutions possess this attribute. The practice of giving back requires that the leader be aware of the social and cultural risks of those around him or her. Charity fuels essential services for those whose legitimate needs might otherwise go unnoticed—and unmet. This is the type of stewardship that can create genuine balance between self-interest and social responsibility.

Charitable behavior can be turned to the advantage of an organization that uses it effectively. It is possible to do well while doing good. An apparel company known to many people allows workers to take a full week off with pay each year to help local charities. The company encourages high-profile executives to participate in charitable bike-a-thons. It also offers four paid sabbaticals each year, for up to six months, for employees who agree to work full-time at a non-profit charity. This amount of favorable publicity costs far less than the dollars that would be required to purchase comparable advertising and public relations. To make the story even better, every phase of generosity that the company is promoting fits within the culture of that company to give back to the community.[1]

It is not our position to encourage one organization to copy another. Charitable giving is a reflection of corporate and organizational citizenship. Charity is about the establishing of and support for facilities and activities that enhance opportunities for others. Integrity-centered organizations act upon the assumption that they owe the communities in which they prosper whatever assistance is required to protect those who cannot protect themselves. This about boys' and girls' clubs; family service agencies; rehabilitative programs, and sometimes simply food and shelter.

Integrity-centered individuals realize that we never stand as tall as when we bend down to help a child. So, too, this profound insight applies to those who lead our free market system. Leaders and organizations with integrity communicate an attitude or culture of giving back to the community, of providing essential services for those in need. Further, it is in everyone's interest to teach powerful lessons that are best communicated by example; none more important than the attribute of charity. When giving is provided by the gracious efforts of those who care, the community itself is made stronger.

NOTES

1   *Career Journal*, Wall Street Journal, September 9, 2003. Dow Jones & Company.

Chapter 11
GRACIOUSNESS:
Respect and Discipline

I shall pass through this world but once.
Any good thing therefore that I can do, or any kindness
that I can show to any human being, let me do it now.
Let me not defer it or neglect it, for I shall not pass this way again.
— Etienne de Grellet

Many people would describe "graciousness" as the art of behaving in a kind and gentle manner. As far as this definition goes, it is accurate. But within the context of integrity, there is more to graciousness. Graciousness demonstrates care and concern for all stakeholders, in both profound and simple ways. The profound aspect of gracious behavior is reflected in the act of nurturing relationships—at work or at home. Graciousness is the art of allowing others to feel valued. Gracious behavior is a sign of respect.

In a business context, an example of graciousness might be as simple as preparing conference spaces so that each participant has a clear view of every aspect of a meeting, including fellow participants. This level of sensitivity also includes taking into consideration additional needs such as beverages, napkins, writing materials and comfortable seating. On the personal side, graciousness can be as powerful as helping children understand immediately that they are much more valuable than the light-color carpet they have just stained with grape soda. Likewise, employees need to understand that they are more important than the machine that was just broken, or the message that was lost. An integrity-centered organization adopts policies that ensure that minor issues never become obstacles, interfering with relationships upon which the organization depends.

The relationship between integrity and graciousness is clear: Gracious behavior is needed everywhere and at all times. Indeed, graciousness is even more important when we are confronted with uncomfortable or unpleasant situations. Minor irritations (such as nighttime interruptions by telemarketers) also require a gracious response, as is discussed in the following letter.

Dear Jim:

My telephone still rings, night after night, with pushy telemarketers. I thought some laws were passed that had put a stop to their calls. But, they still call when we are eating dinner and sometimes after we have gone to bed. I work an early shift and sometimes am exhausted by 9:00 p.m.; and they call as late as 9:40 at night. Being awakened by a computer-dialed phone is ridiculous. What kinds of people expect others to buy from them when they are constantly hounding us at night? Isn't there something wrong with their integrity when they operate like this? I don't even want them to call me and I am not sure how to get rid of them. Slamming the phone down is wrong, but what else can I do? My own way of treating people does not allow me to be rude, but this type of abuse is wrong. Can you help me?

Response:

The telemarketing industry has become more aggressive in recent years. Its intensity and insensitivity have caused many of its potential clients and customers to react in ways similar to your own. You are not alone in being frustrated and irritated by their intrusive and incessant calling. They have seemed to be operating without any regard to the consumers. Comedians have made jokes about this process and have suggested placing the receiver of the phone down, after they interrupt your evening, and indicate that you need to pick up a pencil and paper, only to ignore them until the line goes dead—wasting their time and reducing your stress by not listening to them.

Humorous as this might appear, it is not a proper response; certainly it is not integrity-centered. Such tempting behavior is not gracious. Those who are working for a telemarketing firm need to find customers. This is how they are trying to make a living and it is not appropriate to make their lives miserable because their approach is making our lives miserable. And even if we are upset that they are wasting our time, still we ought not to get back at them with a time-wasting prank.

There is a better way, really an integrity-centered way, to handle unwanted phone solicitation. ... on October 1, 2003, a new law [went] into effect as a part of the "National Do Not Call Registry," and it will fine telemarketers as much as $11,000 each time they call someone listed on the Federal do-not-call listing. The Federal Trade Commission is offering a toll-free number and access to a Website to stop the calls. Here is how to register with the Do Not Call Registry: (888) 382-1222; or register through the Web at: www.donotcall.gov

According to a Los Angeles Times news story, "Telemarketers Brace for The List," written by David Streitfeld [and published on August 24, 2003], the telemarketers are pleased with this new regulation. At least that is what the spokespeople are saying. They say it will greatly simplify their operations by drawing a line between those who don't want to be called and all the others, who the telemarketers will assume are eager to talk. Some of the major telemarketers support the registry because they say that they believe in the consumers' right to be left alone.

These organizations, however, have lobbyists who feel differently. The American Teleservices and Direct Marketing associations have filed lawsuits to stop the registry, which they say is a violation of free speech. They also say that the registry will ruin the telemarketing industry.

Because the telemarketing industry did not regulate itself, (it became too intrusive and abusive of people's time at home, especially during the evening), then the government stepped in with a legislative response—specifically, the Do Not Call Registry. The people, you and others, know that when free markets do not regulate themselves, then those frustrations will be communicated to those in authority, essentially asking and demanding the necessary controls be instituted by the government. Here is an instance where our government has responded with controls and regulations.

Self-regulation and graciousness, seemingly an absent combination in the telemarketing industry, are desirable attributes. Dr. Leonard J. Fletcher (a special advisor for one of the authors) was an individual who embodied these two behaviors. The following anecdote about how Dr. Fletcher and his wife, Ruth, kept personal frustrations in perspective, introduces the concept of the "Nickel Philosophy" (see page 152) and describes how it was developed.

Once a senior executive of a widely known public company, Dr. Fletcher was known for his intelligence, effectiveness and graciousness. He was 88 when the following events occurred.

He and his spouse of 60 years, Ruth, had collected souvenir china tea cups from various cities throughout the world. Routinely, the Fletchers would use these cups when entertaining guests. A visitor provided one such opportunity. Dr. Fletcher selected a tea cup from the collection, and was bringing tea to his visitor when he stumbled and dropped the cup, which then shattered. It was a mess. His visitor correctly guessed that this particular cup was irreplaceable. Dr. Fletcher's wife rushed into the room to find out what had happened. The visitor waited for the predictable and understandable frustrations from either Dr. Fletcher or his wife, but none came. Instead, Ruth, seeing what had happened and that no one was hurt, said, "Oh, Leonard. Oh, Fletch, it's only a Five." Dr. Fletcher then excused himself with an apology, explaining, "I'm sorry, Ruth, I stumbled on the carpet," and then with a smile, he calmly picked up the remnants of the cup and put them in the trash. He then obtained another, similar, cup and served the tea a second time.

Just before noon, it came time for Dr. Fletcher and his wife to take the visitor to lunch. When Dr. Fletcher backed his car out of the garage, he struck a post at the rear of the driveway and crumpled the rear bumper and right rear fender rather badly. The angle of impact can result in an unusually high level of damage from a low-impact collision; such was the case here. Dr. Fletcher immediately examined the damage. His wife, who was in the back seat, told him, "It's a Five!" With that, he returned to the car and smiled, ready to proceed despite the damage. The visitor watched and listened in a state of confused fascination.

In fact, he was astounded. "Fletch," the visitor said, "what is this you and Ruth are saying and smiling about when you say, 'It's a Five'? First, there was the broken tea cup, and now you have damaged your car. I know little about fixing cars, but the damage must be several thousands of dollars, and that tea cup cannot be easily replaced, if at all. Yet you and your wife both say, 'It's a Five,' and go on about your business. Are you speaking in some code? What am I missing? What is going on?"

Dr. Fletcher explained, "That cup and the car are minor issues. The cup is representative of a memory, which we still have, and the car is insured and can be repaired. I am not as good a driver as I used to be and don't see in the shadows very well. I don't like that, but the alternative to getting older is not very attractive." He looked at his visitor, and said, "In our set of priorities, these little accidents stand far behind our relationship with God, or with each other, with our families, and our health. Our social relationships, such as our time with you, and not to mention our economic well-being, are much more important. In other words, the cup and the fender are of such minor importance, we call them 'Fives.'" He went on, "Years ago, Ruth and I sat down and developed our priorities for our life, and agreed that we would never make minor issues more important than higher priority items. This has served us well." With a wink, he said, "And we encourage others to do the same."

Dr. Fletcher was the visitor's mentor. The visitor (and his wife) took that advice and developed their own values set, which they called their "Nickel Philosophy." In turn, it became the foundation that led to the development of the Nickel Philosophy of Dimension Five Consultants, Inc., the organization that nurtures the working lives of the authors. The Nickel Philosophy is shown on the following page.

When we speak of Dr. Fletcher, we do so with appreciation and admiration. Thanks to his guidance, we have the Nickel Philosophy to read, study and apply. Many of the irritations of life are simply "Fives" when measured against genuinely important things.

The value and application of "It's a Five!" to the subject of graciousness is straightforward. If we have perspective and learn not to take small things too seriously, we will tend not to over-react to situations and thereby intrude on the well-being of other people.

Some years ago, an executive (let's call him "Harry") and his family arrived at a hotel near the San Francisco International Airport after a grueling trip from Asia. It was still morning, during the hotel's transition time, perhaps an hour before check-out for the previous night's guests, and two hours before check-in. Harry, no doubt tired from traveling, inquired from the front desk clerk if he might get his room at that time. He was scheduled to have a luncheon meeting, and wanted to freshen up. The clerk informed Harry that the rooms were not yet prepared. Harry lost his composure; he wanted his room—"Now!" He berated the clerk and the hotel in a loud voice, informing the world that he had specified "early arrival" upon making the reservation. He used inappropriate language, and engaged in what could only be called a "temper tantrum." Of course, all of this was witnessed by the very person Harry had wanted to meet before the larger group convened. Let's call the key person "Peter." Peter had just rounded the corner of the hotel lobby and witnessed Harry's meltdown in full force.

We know that Harry is normally a gentle person, and this tirade was not typical behavior. But the hotel employees did not know that, and Peter was not sure. Peter waited for things to quiet down, and for Harry's family to make their way to the coffee shop. He then made his presence known to Harry, asking him, "...would you like to postpone our meeting until later?" Harry paled, and asked, "How long have you been waiting?" To which Peter said, "Long enough. I

The Nickel Philosophy©

PRIORITIES

Professional Profits

1. Customer Service
2. Quality Product
3. Career Opportunity
4. Motivating Environment

YOU

5. The Little Things*

*Petty irritations, not an irreversible economic crisis.

Personal Values

1. Self/Significant Other
2. Family and Friends
3. Health and Happiness
4. Difference and Dollars

5. The Little Things*

*Pebbles between our toes, not boulders on the pathway.

There are times when we feel upset, even "miffed." Toast does get burned. Appointments are cancelled. Bosses neglect the lubricating magic of praise. Children forget, while parents remember. Memos and messages sometimes miscommunicate.

So, what are we to do? For some it means becoming angry. Others seize such opportunities not only to get angry, but also to get even. Such responses are seldom productive.

Therefore, the **Nickel Philosophy** suggests that we calculate the costs of being upset. As often as possible, let's make the petty problems into "5's." That means we identify little issues for what they are: petty irritations, not worthy of much time and energy. Certainly these "5's" do not deserve the attention we lavish on them with our angry responses and hurt feelings. By saying "It's *only* a 5!" we are letting those about us know we understand. They will feel better and so will we. Saying "It's a 5!" is a sure way to keep friends, build morale, and improve productivity.

DIMENSION FIVE

observed you at the front desk. Are you sure this is how you want the hotel staff to remember you?" Embarrassed, Harry realized at once the impression he had made, excused himself and went to the front desk to apologize to the clerk. Upon returning, he apologized to Peter again, explaining how tired he was. Both agreed that the behavior was unacceptable. Peter commented that it would be well for both of them to also remember that in a public place, a person can lose a hard-won reputation for graciousness and professionalism with a single outburst, particularly as there is no way to know who is witnessing the situation.

Now, one can only hope that episode has served both men very well, providing a reminder of how important gracious behavior is—first, because it is the right way to behave; and second, because it is good business to treat others well.

There are times when it is both naïve and wise to assume that people mean well, even when one cannot be certain. The trade-off would seem to be that it is healthier to live with a few disappointments rather than to face the stresses associated with the constant assessment of others' motives. The latter activity has the potential to become a self-fulfilling prophecy, wherein the accompanying suspicion sours a relationship before it has a chance to develop. Gracious behavior is informed, at least to a certain extent, by a gracious attitude; this point is illustrated in the following exchange with an "Integrity Matters" reader.

> Dear Jim:
>
> Earlier today, I pulled into the car wash, rolled down my window and requested their ten-dollar service. The efficient attendant, a young woman, was smiling, and then came the bomb. She asked if I was qualified for the senior citizen's discount. Not knowing how to respond, and being in my mid-fifties, I asked what age one needed to be for the discount. When she said 65, I wondered how beat up and tired I looked. Should this question be asked? Is this business operating with integrity when it allows employees to risk embarrassing folks with age-sensitive questions and assumptions?

> Response:
>
> So, you look a little older than you had thought. Do you remember how old that people who were even 45 looked when you were quite young? Was her question about your age intended to intrude upon your privacy or be attentive to ways her company might help you to save a few dollars? For the number of times this question about senior citizen discount qualification steps on toes, there are probably ten times more

instances when the customer appreciates the concern and the thoughtfulness of the car wash ownership.

The integrity issue is yet to be assessed. Since our column speaks of ... integrity-centered attributes, let's review this event and make note, with [italics], of how behaviors can be surveyed against standards of appropriate conduct. What really matters in this situation is not so much the young person's question about age, but rather your response. Did you accept the discount, knowing you did not deserve it? The integrity-centered response is the truth. You are not 65 and ought not to accept the offer. If you did, were you being *honest*? No.

Pushing ego aside, were you *gracious* in how you treated the employee? She attempted to assist a person who she believed deserved a little extra attention, financially. She was attempting to be professional and productive. Did you demonstrate respect and discipline with reference to how you responded to this person? Did you thank the person for trying to be helpful? Did you control your own negative emotional reaction, recognizing that your uncertainty and insecurity about your appearance might not accurately reflect the motivations of either the person asking the question or the organization that believes the question about age ought to be asked? Were you kind?

The circumstances in which we find ourselves might not do as much harm to us as can our responses to them. It is not simply what happens; it is how we handle things that reflect our *character*. As the older participant in the encounter, and perhaps even the wiser and more mature individual, were you able to exhibit the right behavior? It is not appropriate to react and shake this employee's confidence. She was doing her job by carrying out her company's policies. She behaved with integrity. Did you?

Obviously, the local car wash is not the only arena for graciousness. We encounter multiple opportunities to demonstrate care and concern for others every day. But even practices that may be acceptable to some people can have an effect on others that lacks grace. These practices should be examined when encountered.

The lack of graciousness that permeates our political theater is of particular importance when considered in regard to the restoration of trust. Our elected leaders represent all members of society; everyone is a stakeholder. Society needs integrity-centered leaders who focus on the greater good—not on personal power and prestige. Unfortunately, it has become the practice to attack the reputation of opponents in preference to taking an identifiable stand on the issues. This situation generated the following letter from an "Integrity Matters" reader.

> Dear Jim:
>
> Why have political campaigns become so dirty? Why do we put up with politicians who seek to destroy opponents?

Response:

> Because a significant segment of our society enjoys wallowing in filth. We are witness to a proliferation of smut and violence in many segments: television, movies, comedy, music and writing.
>
> Political activities reflect a world that worships conquerors vanquishing opponents. The positive difference in modern times may be that we no longer literally kill those whom we defeat. We humiliate them, embarrass their families and hire "dirty trick" specialists to distribute disinformation (lies) about their records.
>
> When we choose to reward dignity with respect, and social service with loyalty and honor, we will likely attract a higher caliber process. Until then, take your gas mask to the voting booth and elect the lesser smelling stench.

There are many people elected to public office who hold high standards of conduct, and who do not stoop to personality attacks in order to keep their jobs. But the concept of graciousness applies beyond the campaign trail. Our political leaders are held to high standards, as are leaders in all fields, and sometimes they let us down in ways that are surprising and disappointing. Such an instance occurred during the winter of 2002–2003, when Senator Trent Lott (then the Republican Majority Leader in the U.S. Senate) made insensitive remarks during a toast in honor of the 100th birthday of Senator Strom Thurmond. Concern over this issue brought the following letter from an "Integrity Matters" reader.

> Dear Jim:
>
> Trent Lott has apologized for his implied segregationist view. Many won't forgive him. Others insist he stay in power. Some Black leaders are inclined to give him the benefit of the doubt. Still, the Republican political agenda is at risk. The stature of the Republican Party is at risk. In your view, what should be done to restore the integrity of the Party? "Can this man be saved?"

Response:

> The Trent Lott furor was created by a lack of accountability. The public conduct of those who are in leadership roles is subject to examination for consistency between and among actions, words and responsibilities. When individuals in leadership positions exhibit behaviors that expose their flaws, they have undermined their leadership authority. In the business world, responsible boards of directors remove those executives. To retain them would expose the organization to unnecessary financial risk. Should we expect anything less from our elected officials?
>
> Inconsistencies between words and deeds are human, quickly understood and often forgiven with an apology. However, fundamental deficiencies raise serious questions. Can such individuals be trusted with responsibility–whether in spiritual life, business or government? Leaders recognize when they have broken a trust, and take immediate steps to correct the problem. First, they acknowledge their mistakes. Second, they take corrective measures immediately. Finally, if leaders lose their followers as a result, the work for which they were responsible may be compromised, and they step down graciously.
>
> Leaders step down out of respect to their followers and colleagues, and devote ongoing efforts to repair the effects of their errors. Leaders mentor associates to help them avoid similar mistakes. As a consequence, regardless of the profession, leaders owe their followers integrity–so that society can be sustained by a balance between self-interest and social responsibility. It is not only what you have done to get into trouble, but also what you do to get out of trouble that counts. There are consequences for mistakes–even for the powerful.

No doubt Mr. Lott was simply trying to be gracious to retiring Senator Thurmond, but in the process he chose words that were anything but gracious to a large segment of our society. In fact, the populace took such great offense to Mr. Lott's comments that he was finally compelled to resign his leadership role as a result of this episode.

As the previous example demonstrated, graciousness can sometimes be violated to an extent that words cannot repair the damage that has been done. Unfortunately, insensitivity can be expressed numerous ways. The invasion of privacy is a facet of insensitivity that is sometimes reflected by the behavior of the modern media. The following letter (and response) discusses just how serious this situation has become, and how reform is greatly needed.

Dear Jim:

As a former TV news anchor in both the Miami and Los Angeles markets, I am well aware that the media prioritizes and slants stories to gain maximum viewership. However, I am horrified to see the steps that the networks and news services are taking in their coverage of the war in Iraq to outdo each other. It seems that they are determined to gain, and disperse as much information about our military actions and strategies as possible. Every network has a correspondent with some sort of camera at the front. Each network or cable operation has military experts detailing and anticipating our war plans. It seems to me that the safety of our soldiers doesn't factor into what information is put out over the airwaves for everyone, including our enemies, to see. I feel powerless to do anything about this situation, but since you provide a forum for issues of integrity, I wanted to at least vent to someone who might care.

Response:

Integrity may not be the issue regarding tactical battlefield reporting. In fact, we can only hope that information that reaches the public never places the men and women of our armed services in jeopardy.

Of greater concern, however, is the lack of integrity shown by some highly placed celebrity news anchors who, in their slanted speculations about events, motivations and strategies, could undermine the legitimacy of our leadership, inadvertently provide strategic insight for our enemy, and otherwise give aid and comfort to that enemy. Throughout the media, it can be difficult to distinguish between the objective delivery of news (reporting) and the attempt to influence thought (editorial and commentary).

Worse still, unscrupulous and perverse members of our media, in their misguided efforts to "scoop" the competition, have exposed to American families the wartime slaughter of their sons and daughters on television before the next-of-kin notification process had an opportunity to assure simple human dignity. Recently, a case in point from the Associated Press (by Sandra Marquez) regarding a Southern Californian El Monte High School graduate, Jorge A. Gonzalez, who upon graduation, joined the Marines:

> Rosa and Mario Gonzalez were flipping through TV channels on Sunday [March 23, 2003] when they saw footage of an Iraqi soldier showing off the dead body of an American serviceman.

When they took a closer look, they thought they recognized the body as their son, Marine Cpl. Jorge A. Gonzalez.

"I said to myself, it's not him," Mario Gonzalez said Wednesday. "All day Sunday, we were in shock. We would close our eyes and see those images. ..."

The parents said they saw their son on footage originally shown on the Arab network Al-Jazeera that was rebroadcast on Spanish-language Telemundo on Sunday. In the footage, four bodies could be seen lying on the floor of a room.

Over the weekend, Al-Jazeera aired video footage provided by the Iraqi government that showed dead and captured soldiers. At least two of the interviewed prisoners said they were with the Army's 507th Maintenance Company, part of the 111th Air Defense Artillery Brigade.

The footage was broadcast around the world. U.S. networks initially declined to show it, but some have since shown parts of the tape that does not reveal identifying features.

News coverage that is live 24 hours a day faces incredible challenges. This coverage must be enticing and informative, yet simultaneously attract sponsors whose objectives are to sell products and services. Herein we find the difficulty. When push comes to shove, will news organizations choose to supply us with important news? Market share seems to influence the shape of the news reporting. Cash casts a giant shadow.

Our media supply lots of interesting stories, but not necessarily important information. Further, when the public demands sensational stories rather than enlightening information, reporting will likely respond to the "want to know" mentality instead of the "essential to know." Add the economic pressure of attracting advertising dollars to our society's incredible appetite for gobbling up stories and tidbits of fascinating and sensational news, and one is confronted by a competitive stage ripe for abuse, indecision and irresponsibility. When the mass audience applauds and the writers of current events respond with their media magic, then we may be presented with the sensational and superficial at the expense of the substantive and the important.

"Reality shows" (and sensational stories) that celebrate our lowest instincts deliver little long-term value. When a certain Middle-Eastern television enterprise passed along horrible films of the murder and torture of our military personnel, most broadcast networks decided not to "air" the material. Some, however, decided that we ought to view the horror. This is not ethical journalism; it is [terrible] sensationalism!

The responsibility of a news reporting organization is not entertainment. Giving to people what they want (and beg for) may not always be what is wisest. Consider the alcoholic begging for another drink or the drug abuser seeking one more "high." If the media, electronic and print, cannot determine how best to regulate themselves (on behalf of the society that bestows freedom of the press), then they jeopardize the very foundations of our society! Our column, "Integrity Matters," has addressed abuses by many enterprises. Over and over, we caution individuals and institutions to govern their own behaviors. The very same must be said about the media: "It should be common knowledge that free markets [including the media] must regulate themselves or governments will."

Seemingly, everyone wants to know how best to remain a productive citizen, and our media can help through responsible reporting of events. They can communicate a sense of proportion in how stories are presented and refuse to get caught up in the rush to sensationalize the news. In the final analysis, integrity matters.

Gracious behavior—treating others with thoughtfulness and respect—must become the norm if we are to restore the trust in the leaders of our institutions. The level and quality of care and concern for others is a demonstration of graciousness and a confirmation of integrity-centered relationships. How can trust exist if we do not demonstrate care for others? How can trust exist if we do not show concern for others? How can our society be expected to become more gracious when those to whom we turn for leadership and guidance do not exhibit gracious behavior? Graciousness is the lubricant—and the mortar—for relationships, and includes those "little, nameless, unremembered acts of kindness and of love" (a phrase from British poet William Wordsworth). Gracious acts sustain the integrity-centered enterprise.

Chapter 12

A CASE IN POINT:
Salinas Valley Agribusiness

By the reed bridge that arched the flood,
their flag to April's breeze unfurled,
here once the embattled farmers stood,
and fired the shot heard 'round the world.
– Ralph Waldo Emerson

In the challenge to rebuild our nation's trust in the leadership of its institutions, the equivalent of Emerson's "Shot heard 'round the world" may have already been fired from the Salinas Valley in central California.

The Salinas Valley is in Monterey County and is located about 100 miles south of San Francisco, adjacent to the Monterey Peninsula. It is a fertile agricultural center that rests between the Santa Lucia and Gabilan mountain ranges, following the Salinas River to its opening into the Pacific Ocean at Monterey Bay. The city of Salinas is also the county seat, and home of the National Steinbeck Center (celebrating the life and literary contributions of local son and award-winning author John Steinbeck). The city has about 150,000 residents. Salinas agribusiness generates approximately $3 billion annually. It is one of our nation's most productive "salad bowl" farm centers, labeled by Steinbeck as the "Valley of the World." Traveling through, one sees thousands of acres devoted to row-crop vegetables such as lettuce, asparagus, artichokes and strawberries.

Those who know the region's agricultural leaders describe their operating culture as one of fair dealing; a culture that is reminiscent of values exhibited by those who founded the United States. In December 2002 we began discussing the topic of values and leadership with Basil Mills, President of Mills, Inc., a produce grower-shipper based in Salinas. He was concerned with passing along important values to future generations (the children of today's leaders, as well as those who would join with them, and those who would lead in the future) in the best manner possible. Mills' focus was on agribusiness; ours was on national and regional leadership. We discovered similar concerns regarding who would carry on the ethical practices from the past to ensure the stability of leadership in Salinas Valley agribusiness, and realized we needed to study the situation further.

We quickly learned about the temptation to forsake some of the traditional integrity within the agricultural industry. Two reasons for this situation were suggested: the sale of local grower-shipper businesses to large multinational corporations beholden to quarterly earnings reports, and feelings of entitlement among some of the maturing children of the leadership families in the Salinas-area agribusiness industry. Was there some way, we wondered together, that the values of the early leaders who had made Salinas agribusiness successful might be passed on to the next generation of leaders?

Of principal interest to Mills has been preserving something he has experienced over his 50-year career: the tradition of the "verbal handshake," a shorthand expression that refers to the trust relationship among the various companies in the Salinas Valley agribusiness industry. This relationship had its origins among the early grower-shippers of row-crop vegetables, an industry that began to develop in the 1920's. Today, millions of dollars in business agreements are conducted with a phone call or handshake among the area's agribusiness leaders, who, at various times (and, on occasion, simultaneously) deal with one another as suppliers, buyers and competitors. Obviously, they work in an industry where the products are highly perishable. Produce has a shelf life measured in days and weeks; growers simply do not have time for lengthy contractual negotiations during the harvest. Furthermore, as they cannot pack up their land and move it elsewhere, the growers all know that they will be working together (in one capacity or another) again and again. The long view of those who are successful in the Salinas Valley, then, is simple: trust—and trustworthiness.

We studied Mills' question (Who would carry on the ethical traditions of the past to ensure stable leadership in Salinas Valley agribusiness?) and, in further discussions with him, we concluded that it would make sense to gather leaders of various agribusiness companies in the Salinas Valley to see if they shared his concerns. We also wanted to learn if they could help to find a solution. As a result, in early 2003, Mills invited 17 fellow agribusiness leaders to discuss foundational values that had been present at the launching of row-crop farming in the Salinas Valley.

Gathering several times in various groupings over a five-month period to document the values of the early leaders, attendees responded to Mills' initial concerns. The values could be summarized. New generations could be taught.

These conversations were designed to build an integrity-centered platform for future generations so that they might be even better stewards of both land and values. Mills and his colleagues felt that by equipping the next generation of leaders with the previous leaders' work ethic, sense of history, stewardship and social responsibility, the recipients of this "proud heritage" would be more likely to carry on the best of the traditions. Successful succession is seldom accidental.

As early as the 1920's and 1930's, the early leaders of Salinas Valley agriculture (as we know it today) demonstrated integrity-centered business principles with their "verbal handshake agreement" approach and generous commitment to community. Their mutual respect and tenacious cooperation, coupled with their competitiveness for both growth and innovation, laid the groundwork for Salinas Valley agribusiness to become the "Valley of the World" (this phrase is also the theme of the agricultural wing of the National Steinbeck Center).

Remembering all that was good and could be good again, current leaders decided to create a values-based succession plan, named "The Salinas Valley Agribusiness Integrity-Centered Leadership Program." Again, building upon early leaders' principles, a cooperative association was established between and agribusiness leadership, the National Steinbeck Center and the Bracher Center for Integrity in Leadership to carry forward these values and the sense of history for future leaders. This Program was formulated from the collaborative efforts of this association.

The choice of the National Steinbeck Center as the meeting place of agribusiness leaders reveals another important trait of the Salinas Valley agribusiness leadership—understanding and respect for historical values. Steinbeck, a Nobel Laureate, was born in Salinas in 1902 and wrote numerous books, short stories and screenplays. He is recently remembered through the recommendation of his 1952 book, *East of Eden*, by the Oprah Winfrey Book Club in September 2003. Steinbeck is perhaps best remembered for his controversial novel, *The Grapes of Wrath*, published in 1939, which was a fictionalized account of the migrant farm worker's plight during the Depression years of the 1930's. The book generated an enormous social reaction as well as tremendous criticism in the Salinas Valley at the time of publication. Many Salinas Valley leaders of that era rejected the picture painted by Steinbeck in *The Grapes of Wrath*. It is a confirmation of the integrity of current community leaders that the grower-shippers of the Salinas area today not only utilize the National Steinbeck Center for some of their meetings, but several also serve on the organization's Board of Directors. These second- and third-generation leaders have also helped significantly with the Center's funding. This speaks well of the progress made by the people and their opinion leaders over the years, and of the insight and openness of those who lead Salinas Valley agribusiness today.

The efforts of current Salinas Valley agribusiness leaders were recognized by Scott Faust, Executive Editor of *The Californian*, in an article published in that newspaper on August 6, 2003 (excerpts reprinted below).

Ag execs agree on ethics principles
Salinas Valley effort underscores values

A six-month effort to identify core values of Salinas Valley agriculture has yielded a set of principles that organizers say could foster a nationwide renewal of business ethics.

At a meeting in Salinas on Monday, ag executives heralded the moral legacy of those who established the local produce industry in the 1920s and '30s. Today, the multibillion-dollar sector–led by many of their descendants–directly or indirectly employs more than 30 percent of Monterey County's workforce.

One concept emphasized throughout an agreed-upon document is that of a "verbal handshake" — the mutual trust that permits quick transactions under the deadlines of a perishable commodity. Also emphasized is the idea of giving back to the community, which participants say is still reflected in the civic generosity of many ag companies in such causes as Relay for Life, the annual fund-raiser for cancer research.

Richard Green/The Californian file photo

Jim Bracher, center, conducts brainstorming on agribusiness ethics June 12 at the National Steinbeck Center.

"In many of the families, fathers have taught their sons and daughters these things, but there's no guarantee that's going to go on as we bring so many new people into this industry."
— Basil Mills, founder of Mills, Inc.

Longtime ag executive Basil Mills, who joined with Monterey business consultant Jim Bracher to launch the values program, said a primary goal was to reinforce basic ethics among the next generation of industry leaders.

"You don't always get these things by osmosis," said Mills, founder and president of Mills, Inc., a Salinas-based produce firm. "In many of the families, fathers have taught their sons and daughters these things, but there's no guarantee that's going to go on as we bring so many new people into this industry."

Training may follow

Formally known as the Salinas Valley Agribusiness Integrity-Centered Leadership Program, the effort's next step will be a trial run of a training curriculum based on eight key values that include such things as honesty, openness and performance.

Mills said Tuesday he expects a small group of top ag executives this fall to try out an industry-specific course that could later be presented to promising leaders within local agribusiness companies.

They will include some of the 17 participants who attended about five meetings since March at the National Steinbeck Center, which also was represented in the discussions. The agribusiness integrity principles may eventually be displayed in some way at the Steinbeck Center's new Agricultural History and Education Center, scheduled to open Sept. 1.

The 17 included many prominent figures: Bill Ramsey, co-board chairman of Mann Packing Co.; Bob Antle, co-chairman of Tanimura & Antle; and Jim Bogart, president of the Grower-Shipper Association of Central California.

Bracher, who is founder and president of the Bracher Center for Integrity in Leadership, said he's hopeful the ag-focused training program he coordinated will make the Salinas Valley a national model.

Though he did not charge participants a fee as facilitator, he said he would like to take the basic approach to core business values and market it to other industries as a moneymaking venture.

"Sowing the seeds for the renewal of free markets is the essence of what drove me to it," said Bracher, who first approached Mills with the concept in January. "The more we discover about it (Salinas Valley agribusiness), the more we believe this is the legitimate home for the renewal of free enterprise."

Mills cited the raft of corporate-ethics scandals that have made headlines over the past year, including such big names as Enron, WorldCom and Global Crossing.

He said the newly agreed-upon agribusiness principles do not mean that industry leaders consider their companies incapable of missteps.

"Really, the country is crying out for something like this," Mills said. "... None of us is immune to forgetting some of the basic things that are important: integrity, fairness and how we treat people, whether they're customers or employees."

Companies rated

One thing that sets the produce industry apart from other businesses is a pair of private rating systems called The Blue Book and The Red Book. Both include financial and character ratings based on information provided by companies about themselves and their peers.

Jim Carr, president/CEO of the Produce Reporter Company, the Illinois-based firm that owns The Blue Book, said he's not aware of any effort quite like the values standards just agreed upon by Salinas Valley ag leaders.

"The people in the Salinas area are very good," said Carr, who also teaches business ethics at Wheaton College in Wheaton, Ill. "Many of the companies are very good — very highly rated by our firm."

Perhaps the youngest participant in the values-agreement process was Lorri Koster, daughter of Don Nucci, Ramsey's co-chairman at Mann Packing.

Koster, who owns her own ag-related communications firm, said some observers may overlook the importance of character and honesty in the success of early agribusiness leaders.

"Innovation certainly made the companies successful," she said, "but it was also how they were managed."

Jerry Esquivel, a second-generation agri-businessman who did not take part in the values-brainstorming effort, said he has found that written agreements are more and more important, despite close-knit relationships.

"You don't want to be left hanging with a payroll of employees after you've harvested a 30-acre field," said Esquivel, co-owner of Chieftain Harvesting.

But he said he's not ready to give up on cherished ideals.

"It would be nice to have the old-school ethics the way we grew up," Esquivel said, "where word of mouth and a handshake really went a long way."

At a glance

The following are the eight key values of the Salinas Valley Agribusiness Integrity-Centered Leadership Program, adopted Monday by a committee of 16 leaders of valley agricultural companies. Listed with each is a quote from a five-page summary document:

- **Character:** "Business is transacted with a phone call or a handshake, and even though much of agribusiness today involves contracts, it is clear that contracts are formalities..."

- **Honesty:** "From the irrigator and harvester in the field to the broker and the shipper in the office, every person must understand that agribusiness as a whole thrives on honest and reliable information exchange."

- **Openness:** "Openness with competitors, perhaps unusual in other industries, is routine in agribusiness. While it is a competitive business, it is interdependent and cannot prosper without openness."

- **Authority:** "The early leaders and their successors have succeeded in building a climate of authority based on performance, knowledge, competence, follow-through and trust."

- **Partnership:** "They have developed business relationships where any company can be the competitor, the supplier and the customer of the other company."

- **Performance:** "Today's leaders will need entrepreneurial spirit and common sense, along with the drive and energy necessary to persevere with high standards of ethical performance."

- **Charity:** "Stewardship begins with the land and extends to the citizens who share responsibility for making the soil productive."

- **Graciousness:** "The early leaders of the Salinas Valley agribusiness community could be seen performing alongside their employees, as no job was too small nor any person unimportant."

Following the publication of this article, Jim Carr, the President and Chief Executive Officer of the Produce Reporter Co. Inc., the publisher of The Blue Book™ (which, according to the newspaper article previously presented, "provides financial and character ratings based on information provided by the companies about themselves and their peers"), visited the Bracher Center and toured the Steinbeck Center. Carr mentions his visit in the following letter (reprinted with permission).

September 19, 2003

Mr. James F. Bracher, Founder
Bracher Center for Integrity in Leadership
1400 Munras Avenue
Monterey, CA 93940

Dear Jim:

In follow-up to the article in the August 6, 2003, The Californian, entitled, "Ag Execs Agree on Ethics Principles—Salinas Valley Effort Underscores Values," I felt it was appropriate and necessary for me to travel to California, meet with you at the Bracher Center, and tour the National Steinbeck Center in Salinas and see the Valley of the World History and Education Center exhibit. After visiting the Center and you, I firmly believe that your project has significant promise for strengthening business practices and restoring trust throughout business and society.

As the president and CEO of a 102-year-old organization, which lists and rates fresh fruit and vegetable businesses from a financial, ethical and pay description perspective, it was important to discuss with you, firsthand, the Salinas Valley Agribusiness Integrity-Centered Leadership Program. It was valuable to see what members of the produce industry in the Salinas Valley are doing to ensure that its business is conducted in the same ethical manner as those who preceded this generation. The operating principles of those in the Salinas Valley extend outward from their own community and state to the nation and the world.

What you have helped them to formalize, in the way of behaviors to be emulated, is a foundation based on ethical principles that will be an inspiration for others to conduct business in the right way. This project renews my faith in the free-market system!

Especially powerful are the eight attributes developed through the Bracher Center for Integrity in Leadership—character, honesty, openness, authority, partnership, performance, charity and graciousness.

The Center has found a way to describe and illustrate the trading methods which the produce industry has embraced for many years, and which I hope will be clearly articulated when they are displayed in the Valley of the World History and Education Center wing of the National Steinbeck Center.

Wouldn't it be a wonderful world if all business could be transacted in the same way in which people in the produce industry do business— with a "verbal handshake," in which contracts are reached verbally and fulfilled because people believe that an agreement entered into is binding and should be honored?

Adam Smith, a moral philosopher and economist, who wrote the book, *An Inquiry into the Nature and Causes of the Wealth of Nations*, in 1776, described the make-up of free markets and how people should interact with each other. The most celebrated point is the "invisible hand," which holds that a free marketplace will ensure to the greatest extent possible that businesses, operating competitively, will offer the best price, functioning efficiently and productively, and act in ways that will improve the marketplace.

The produce industry is a terrific example of what Adam Smith encouraged in his writing. By operating competitively, yet cooperatively, the marketplace ensures that businesses will be effective, productive and efficient through time-honored contracts in which each person's word must stand the test of time.

Free markets work because men and women want to see them work. If markets do not work, government will initiate laws and regulations which could stifle and confuse the marketplace.

On the other hand, if men and women of goodwill choose to do business the right way for the right reasons, then the free marketplace can be allowed to work as it should. The produce industry is a shining example, and the National Steinbeck Center, through the Valley of the World History and Education Center, clearly demonstrates this wisdom.

Additional training for the produce industry, and for other industries as well, is necessary. Utilizing effective education that honors appropriate values and the concepts that Adam Smith wrote about many years ago could help restore confidence in individual leadership and organizational accountability.

The Blue Book is pleased and proud to have played an important role in helping the produce marketplace operate more effectively and efficiently over our 102-year history. We provide valuable information and other services which enable, rather than hinder, the free flow of information and ensure that contracts have meaning and will be honored in the proper way.

The eight attributes, which the Bracher Center for Integrity in Leadership is bringing into more and more business conversations, will help restore trust to a marketplace that has been battered by scandal and whose structure is threatened.

I wish you well in your future endeavors, and the Blue Book welcomes the opportunity to discuss with you how we might assist to make your eight integrity-centered attributes a part of doing business everywhere, and at all times.

Respectfully,

Produce Reporter Company
C. James Carr
President

What is particularly interesting and relevant to our commitment to restore trust in the leadership of our nation's institutions and businesses is the nature of the Blue Book itself. One of two rating services specific to the fresh fruit and vegetable industry (the other being the Red Book™), the Blue Book has the following statement of purpose:

> The Produce Reporter Company, doing business as Blue Book Services, provides listing, rating, and marketing facts about firms operating in the fresh fruit and vegetable industry, as well as those firms which transport fresh fruits and vegetables, principally within North America, but internationally as well. Firms are rated financially and ethically, and, if they buy and take title to produce, services, or transportation, a pay description is reported. The moral responsibility rating is based on trade responses received from those with whom a business deals, detailing in particular a firm's integrity and ability. The pay description is also determined via trade reports received from those with whom a business deals. Related services provided by Blue Book Services include educational seminars, dispute resolution, and collection services. Blue Book Services was founded in 1901, is privately owned, and enjoys a very favorable reputation through accurate, timely, and reliable services and information assisting businesses to do business productively, efficiently, and profitably.

Two independent mercantile rating services exist for the produce industry. The competitor of the Blue Book, the Red Book Credit Services, is a product of Vance Publishing Corporation, and is affiliated with its weekly publication, *The Packer*, which also covers the produce industry. On August 25, 2003, *The Packer* published a special insert that reported on the grand opening of the Valley of the World History and Education Center wing of the National Steinbeck Center in Salinas. Within this publication, Pete Maturino, President of the United Food and Commercial Workers Union Local 1096, is quoted as saying:

> "They're doing a great job," he said. "They're telling the facts, regardless of whether it's good or bad. They're trying to show the whole picture."

Salinas Valley agribusiness offers us not an announcement of its own saintliness but rather a challenge to remember what once was good and could be good again. We can learn how to define an integrity-centered organization from the following outline of behaviors and goals (which was created as a result of our work with the Salinas agribusiness community).

Salinas Valley Agribusiness Vision
The Integrity-Centered Agribusiness Company
—by the Bracher Center

1. CHARACTER: Consistency Between Word and Deed

   Do the leaders of your organization exhibit congruence between what they say and what they do, as well as what they say about what they did?

   - Verbal handshake agreement
   - Fair business practices
   - Sharing innovation
   - Lead by example
   - Perseverance

2. HONESTY: Truthful Communication

   Do you have confidence that your leaders would never engage in or sanction misrepresentation?

   - Clarity
   - Tell the truth
   - Word is bond
   - Straightforward communications

3. OPENNESS: Operational Transparency

   Is appropriate information about your organization readily available?

   - Accountability
   - Face-to-face relationships
   - Open door
   - Self-regulation

4. AUTHORITY: Employee Encouragement

   Are you able to correct a customer problem? Do you have confidence that your actions will be supported?

   - Risk and reward systems reinforce desired behaviors
   - Responsive and responsible customer service
   - Ongoing programs for developing talent

5. PARTNERSHIP: Honor Obligations

Does your organization pride itself on the timely fulfillment of all commitments?

- Partnering for common cause
- Mentor and invest in one another
- Mutual support
- Share innovation

6. PERFORMANCE: Accountability Throughout the Organization

When individuals, including senior executives, underperform repeatedly, are they given due process and then, if necessary, replaced?

- Performance measures in place, with a tie to brand integrity and consumer marketing
- Controls
- Quality assurance
- Sound decisions over time

7. CHARITY: Generous Community Stewardship

Does your organization reach out to those in need?

- Commitment to serious community investment
- Involvement throughout the organization

8. GRACIOUSNESS: Respect and Discipline

Does your organization demonstrate care and concern for all stakeholders?

- Ethnic and cultural awareness and appreciation
- Compassion and understanding
- Humility (no job is too small, nor any worker unimportant)
- Interpersonal ease

The traditional values of Salinas Valley agribusiness, combined with the self-governing aspect contributed by the Blue Book and the Red Book services, represent an example of a path forward for our free market system. The Salinas Valley agribusiness industry may not be unique, but it is certainly a model worth emulating. The effort of the agribusiness community to perpetuate the early leaders' values for their industry may in fact be planting the seeds for the renewal of time-honored values for our nation. We describe their commitment to integrity-centered leadership as finding practical ways to incorporate commonly held values with uncommon ethical practices that sustain business success and strengthen community. It is no stretch of the imagination to believe their approach to an integrity-centered legacy could launch similar movements elsewhere. This first step could be the "values shot" that needs to be heard all over the United States, and maybe around the world.

Chapter 13

The Road Map to an Integrity-Centered Society

We can all take the hero's journey. It begins with a single step,
the moment we stand up for something we believe in.
– Walter Cronkite

Our focus needs to be on the internal restoration of trust within our national house. We need a plan to put this house in order for the benefit of the children of our children, so that it can become again a shining example of freedom and opportunity for all nations, including our own. Action by action, relationship by relationship, child by child, society's values must be renewed. Left unchecked, structural flaws will destroy the integrity of the system and in turn increase the public's anxiety. Unless we find ways to honor our founding principles and repair the cracks and decay, this house of freedom and free markets could collapse. When uncertainty prevails, how long before people demand that the government restrict the entire social system, including free markets themselves?

In the preceding chapters, we discussed the Eight Attributes and how they contribute to integrity-centered behavior. The time is now to evaluate institutions on the very issue of integrity—before more scandals erupt. We have learned from the readers of "Integrity Matters" columns about the many ways in which our values have deteriorated. In Chapter 12 we provided an example that gives hope and perhaps even a road map for us to follow in what has become a national, and now a global, conversation.

However, if we move too quickly beyond the current challenging times, without reflecting on what has happened to us and our society, we may be tempted to fall back into bad habits. If we "get rich and successful" too easily, yet again, we may miss the opportunity to learn from our mistakes. Like an untreated alcoholic, who rationalizes that "just one little drink" will not hurt and will relax him or her for the moment, we may fall into the trap of drifting, seeking easy answers and abdicating responsibility for integrity-centered actions. Since freedom is what we want, it must never be far from our minds that there can be no freedom without discipline—at least, not for long. Our tasks are clear. We need to restore confidence, a step at a time.

Again and again, we have considered the questions and answers from "Integrity Matters" and have been reminded that character is important, as are the other seven integrity-centered attributes. We believe there is a need to rediscover and recommit to the value system that underlies appropriate and constructive behaviors. What is needed now is a road map to show how trust can be restored in each other and throughout various organizations. Only when ways are found to restore confidence in the structures of society will freedoms and the free market system be protected. The question, now, is where does this journey begin?

The answer is, in the mirror! That is our first step. Ten two-letter words provide wisdom: "If it is to be, it is up to me." This journey begins one person, one family, one community, one nation and one world at a time. Our journey of discovery and renewal will thus move from the individual to the building and care of integrity-centered partnerships with others who share similar values. With them, we move to the third step: establishing our priorities for the restoration of trust. Together, we build and strengthen the integrity of our communities in the fourth step, and then, finally, move to the fifth area to build an integrity-centered process within our society. Let's get started.

Step one is self-awareness and self-knowledge. An example of this is from our own experience as business consultants. Approximately 8,000 executives have participated in our leadership counsel during the past 24 years. For the most part, those who were described as "successful" leaders, and who appeared to be managing their careers with the greatest ease, possessed five traits:

1. They had good minds and an ability to remain focused on whatever task was in front of them.

2. They were strong and could work long hours if necessary.

3. They could communicate clearly and powerfully in writing as well as with the spoken word.

4. They had a strong support system, often a spouse, sometimes a significant other.

5. They had clarity in their beliefs and values, and they knew what was important to them and why.

Recognizing the importance of this fifth trait, we believe in making a substantial and significant effort to clarify an individual's own beliefs and priorities. But it is not enough for an individual to rank his or her priorities in order; it is essential for that person to also understand and communicate the values that hold their priorities together. Self-knowledge increases impact and effectiveness.

We offer this challenge: Consider the following exercise to help clarify your values and priorities. On a blank sheet of paper, write your top personal priorities (some "big picture" possibilities to consider include spouse, family, friends, health, happiness and making a difference as well as making a dollar). When you have created your list of four, five or six top priorities, give careful thought to the values that hold them together. What is it about these values that enables you to better leverage your personal priorities productively?

Turning to the professional side, use another blank page and think clearly about your business or economic priorities. Try to keep a clear separation between your personal life and your world of work. In prioritizing for the working world, some areas to be considered might include the care of customers and clients in addition to the quality of the products and services provided. Consider also the need for career opportunity and the kind of motivating work environment that will keep you active, involved and enthusiastic. When you are engaged in your career and work, what are the elements that hold it together and draw you to your highest level of professional performance and productivity?

If your priorities listing looks something like the Nickel Philosophy (see Chapter 11), then you will know immediately how much can be resolved every day simply by being able to distinguish between what is important and what is not. Step one, self-awareness and self-knowledge, is the launching point for the journey of integrity; it must begin with the individual.

Self-awareness represents the single greatest opportunity to leverage interpersonal integrity and effectiveness. Self-knowledge requires feedback from others, perhaps gained through professional consultation, or from supervisors, colleagues and staff. Self-knowledge is strengthened by the willingness and ability to listen. Listening is step one. Objective behavior information can help leaders recognize their strengths and vulnerabilities, their capacity and potential. Such insights help the individual leader to know when, where and how to function more effectively, and to be more at ease with his or her leadership responsibilities, supervisory roles and organizational relationships. Since each of us is at the least the president of his or her own life, it is important for restoring trust within our society as a whole that each individual accepts the responsibility for self-awareness and interpersonal effectiveness.

Let us not lose sight of the mission, however, which is restoring trust. We are not of much value if all we do is wallow in conflicting perspectives of self-knowledge. Take an accurate reading and prepare to act. Then take action! Since just about everyone must relate to others, it soon becomes obvious that communicating effectively with colleagues is essential. When we learn more efficient ways to understand, appreciate and accommodate diverse operating styles, productivity can be increased. Since the character of most individuals is unlikely to change very much, it is prudent to learn ways to refine listening skills and to increase the speed with which one understands others (interpersonal ease is a trait associated with effectiveness). By so doing, individuals can modify their behaviors to enhance their various relationships, whether at work or at home.

Whenever wise people have reflected upon success, self-knowledge was always the starting point. The ability to build and sustain strong relationships was never far behind. Step two is finding and partnering with the right person and seeking those who share similar values.

An "Integrity Matters" reader asked a question that initiated a values examination. This inquiry led to a response that provides an avenue for our discussion of the path to restore trust.

> Dear Jim:
>
> In your weekly newspaper column, you offer responses to integrity questions in areas that interest me: family issues, neighborhood concerns, economic challenges, political problems, spiritual needs and, even honesty among baseball players. Questions: Where do get your answers? How do you know what is ethical? On what basis do you select the values that support your position? How do your columns reflect your philosophy? I read that you were a clergyman. Does that mean you have a Christian bias?
>
> You have stated on more than one occasion that unless we regulate ourselves, governments will. You have persuaded me that we need to do something, but other than obeying the speed limit and practicing the golden rule, I'm uncertain where, exactly, to begin to help restore values. Is there one best way, or "one thing" as the seasoned actor Jack Palance said in the movie *City Slickers,* that might improve our world?

> Response:
>
> My own answers and responses come out of the clarity and confidence that emerge from the single most important human relationship

possible: a strong and committed marriage partner. A person's opinions are shaped by the particular experiences of his or her life. It is true that my own life encounters and training have brought me to my treasured values. Your reference to the movies brought to mind the award-winning film *A Beautiful Mind*. One way to describe how the connection to values and insight work for me is to talk about that movie, which my wife, Jane, and I found very significant:

Winner of the Academy Award for best film in 2002, *A Beautiful Mind* was directed by the former television child-star Ron Howard. Actor Russell Crowe portrays Dr. John Nash, the math wizard and economic genius, professor from Princeton University, who received the 1994 Nobel Prize. The story of his life was the basis for the film. In addition to Russell Crowe, ... Jennifer Connelly played his loyal and dedicated wife, Alicia. Whatever else the movie communicated, the power of unconditional love was the cradle for the messages offered.

Dr. Nash received the shared Economics Nobel Prize in 1994 for his mathematical discoveries and contributions to game theory, which have impacted 20th century business and economic activity. Most important of all for Dr. Nash was how he remembered the importance of his wife in his successes. When he won the Nobel Prize after decades of struggling with schizophrenia, the most serious and debilitating of the mental illnesses, in his acceptance speech, he talked about his wife's understanding and support. It was his wife, Alicia, who had provided him with context, connection and clarity.

Dr. Nash described himself as a person who has been fortunate enough to tell his story through a newspaper article, book and movie. What he also provided via this movie to the current generation was insight related to the power of key relationships that can be about healing, and how unconditional love can inspire self-renewal.

What makes this story so moving centers in the words he shared, at least in the film version of his life, upon receiving the Nobel Prize at the awards ceremony in Stockholm, Sweden, December of 1994.

Dr. Nash, as portrayed by Russell Crowe, summarized his values, insights and his efforts to build and then rebuild his life with and through the integrity-centered behaviors (love and support) of his wife, Alicia, uttering these 101 words:

I have always believed in numbers, in the equations and logics that lead to reason. And, after a lifetime of such pursuits, I ask: what truly is logic? Who decides reason?

My quest has taken me through the physical, the metaphysical, the delusional and back. And I have made the most important discovery of my career; the most important discovery of my life.

It is only in the mysterious equations of love that any logic or reason can be found.

I am only here tonight because of you (referring obviously to his wife, Alicia).

You are the reason I am. You are all my reasons.

Thank You.

These 101 words, when recast through my own experience, help me to form the basis for increasing the knowledge and awareness essential for restoring trust in society, rebuilding faith in institutions and guiding integrity-centered leadership.

Perhaps you will be challenged to utilize this same process for enhancing ways your thoughts and actions can provide for you the answers and direction required in these complex times. Here is my response to how my life and work have unfolded. My words run parallel to what Dr. Nash said when acknowledging the Nobel Prize. His response served as a guideline:

"I have always believed in the potential of the individual, in the capacity of human beings to achieve and contribute. During decades of encouraging integrity-centered actions, for people to be the best they can be, I ask, What is integrity? Who decides which values support appropriate behaviors?

My quest has taken me to theology, teaching, pastoral care, preaching, leadership counseling and now writing. And I have made the most important discovery of my career, the most important discovery of my life.

It is only in the mysterious equations of interpersonal connection, mutual respect and unconditional love that an integrity-centered life is possible. Restoring trust and confidence in the leadership of any society, regionally or globally, rests upon legitimate interpersonal relationships.

Any credit given to me regarding my constructive impact upon the lives of others was made possible because of the unconditional love provided to me by my wife, Jane, who is my best friend, role model and mentor. Her integrity is the source for any trust-restoring leadership counsel that my efforts were able to provide. For those gifts of support and integrity, I offer my thank you."

The basis of integrity-centered leadership is connection, context and value-clarity. Strong marriages exude this connectedness. Family units understand it and live it. Parents who look with pride, with feelings of accomplishment, upon their child-rearing efforts understand how these multiple dimensions of relationship secure the present and prepare the next generation for the future.

Yes, this movie contains a message. Powerful as its story is about a brilliant professor, it is even more about the wife. Perhaps, *A Beautiful Mind* might be re-titled *A Magnificent Marriage of Partnership, Perseverance and Unconditional Love*. Truly, the husband becomes more and is better because of the right wife. Hopefully, the wife says the same thing. Yet, who among us is not better because of those we call friend and ally?

One powerful summary of important relationships can be seen in the following words about friendship. This poem stands as a centering point for our marriage and our relationship in that it is a reminder that we are better because of the love and acceptance of friends, in this very personal instance, a marriage partner:

Friendship

I love you not only for what you are, but
for what I am when I am with you. I love you
not only for what you have made of yourself,
but for what you are making of me. I love you
for the part of me that you bring out.

I love you for putting your hand into my
heaped-up heart, and passing over all the
foolish and frivolous and weak things which
you cannot help dimly seeing there, and for
drawing out into the light all the beautiful,
radiant belongings, that no one else had looked
quite far enough to find.

I love you for ignoring the possibilities of
the fool and weakling in me, and for laying
firm hold on the possibilities of good in me. I
love you for closing your eyes to the discords
in me, and for adding to the music in me by
worshipful listening.

I love you because you are helping me to
make of the lumber of my life not a tavern but
a Temple, and of the words of my every day
not a reproach but a song.

I love you because you have done more
than any creed could have done to make me
good, and more than any fate could have done
to make me happy. You have done it just by
being yourself. Perhaps that is what being a
friend means after all.

— Author unknown

Friendship, grounded in substantive connections, is built upon integrity and holds together relationships while guiding the proper execution of responsibilities. From friendship comes confidence, courage and commitment. Upon these three characteristics a person can build a life of meaning and impact.

Step three is developing and communicating priorities. A process similar to that described with the Nickel Philosophy (discussed earlier) can be of help. When individuals are clear in their beliefs, clear in communicating these beliefs, as well as in how they approach problem-solving, they have a better chance at being successful. Trust is the by-product of forthright and predictable behavior. When individuals and organizations exhibit clarity and consistency through integrity-centered behaviors, confidence will be restored interpersonally and culturally. Restored confidence is the foundation for productivity and sustains interpersonal relationships, families, communities and free markets.

The fourth step in restoring integrity involves the strengthening of communities. Will we ever again live with the doors to our homes and offices unlocked?

Will neighbors look after the properties of those who live next to them? Does no-fault insurance mean that we are no longer responsible for damages we cause to others? Has the success of American democracy and the wealth created by free markets failed to attract the best talent available and serve the public good? Let us carefully examine what is happening in our society. Consider the example provided in the following question from the "Integrity Matters" column.

> Dear Jim:
>
> In professional team sports, the best players—those with the proper mix of skill and talent—take the field/arena/etc. on "game day," regardless of their color, race and/or religion.
>
> In professional organizations, however, the best "players" do not fill the key positions. Often this is because of their color, race, religion, network and/or affiliation ... not skill and talent.
>
> Is there a reason for the different sets of standards given all the laws and regulations regarding equal opportunity employment and non-discrimination?

Response:

> Your question relates to the manner with which positions are filled. Insecure leaders often fill key positions with "known quantities." Depending upon the priorities of some enterprises, winning is a distant second to harmony and family comfort. How else could one explain the lack of a winning tradition among some sport teams? On the other hand, some leaders prefer to employ friends or socially comfortable "slot fillers" instead of seeking only the most qualified to do the work.
>
> One aspect of this socially sensitive approach is admirable, caring for the less obviously capable. The other side of this "relationship coin" could be described as biased, even discriminatory.
>
> In the meantime, enjoy the winning sports programs that grasp the winning team concept and avoid investing in the capitalists who place productivity and profits after their "good old buddy" network of employing friends and pals, male or female.

Socially biased behavior can be seen as a reflection of the broken values that begin with the individual and permeate the family, the community, the corporation, the government agency and spiritual organization. However, there is a solution. It is not complicated. This fourth step is as straightforward as the promises made by any restaurant waiter or waitress. The food service world needs only to fulfill two promises: 1) serve the food ordered, and 2) do it professionally and with courtesy. A community of trust is built when individuals and organizations fulfill their mutual promises—over and over and over again. In other words, do what you say you are going to do, and tell the truth about what you did. Always. When mistakes happen, acknowledge them and apologize for them, and then avoid repeating them. As we know, this is not rocket science, nor does it need to be drudgery. Forthrightness and accountability are building blocks of integrity-centered behavior: from the top job in the corner office to the front-line employee loading boxes.

Interpersonal relationships that are built upon trust provide the connections that sustain the various communities in which we establish our identities. The following "Integrity Matters" column illustrates ways individuals can strengthen the communities of trust in which they participate every day.

> Dear Jim:
>
> Week after week, your Wednesday "Integrity Matters" column generally responds to questions addressing problems created by individuals who violate standards of integrity and ethics. You describe compromised situations and offer suggestions on ways to address and correct the problems. Yes, that is helpful. Please continue your efforts. But, just for a change of pace, would you please cite examples of people who exhibit integrity?

> Response:
>
> Yes, gladly. Let's start with an optimistic assumption that a significant number of human beings are pretty good. We are confident that people will "come through in the clutch" with honesty and caring. We have read about and we know of travelers who have literally "gone the extra mile" (returning 55 miles in their automobile to a roadside restaurant) to correct a $10 overpayment error made by an employee who miscalculated what was due a customer. Whether the items were expensive or simply of sentimental value, we have heard stories of "strangers" finding and returning lost pieces of jewelry. The generosity and graciousness of the "Good Samaritan" story is not simply a religious illustration that resides in the pages of the Bible. Every day, decent people are conducting themselves with sincerity and integrity and they are not making their actions appear to be any big deal.
>
> Certainly, integrity-centered behavior is not anything earth-shattering or new. [It can be as simple as performing one or more of these nameless acts of kindness:]

1. Motioning for an impatient driver to move ahead or to turn in front.

2. As contrasted to simply providing directions, literally escorting visitors or strangers to their destinations, whether on a campus, in a building or to an actual site.

3. Bending down or sitting down to appear face-to-face with a child when communicating, so as to make the relationship and connection less overwhelming.

4. Waiting graciously for the person who answers the telephone to complete introductory comments before interrupting with questions or requests.

5. Listening attentively to the same story, retold the "umpteenth time" by a forgetful friend, appreciating how important the telling of the story is to the speaker.

6. Commending the communication effectiveness, as well as the efforts, of those about us whose second language is English, but upon whose work we depend.

7. Exercising tolerance, spoken and unspoken, for other points of view, recognizing that two people can draw different conclusions from the same situation.

8. Praising the hard work and sincere effort of those who harvest our food, prepare our meals, keep our automobiles running, deliver our mail, teach us, guide us spiritually, operate transportation systems, provide pure water and protect our society. As you think of others, make the effort to show appreciation.

Let me now cite an example of someone who exhibits integrity. A friend of mine, let's call him Fred, has integrity and he loves to play golf. He and I keep score. We compete with one another, and each of us loves to win. In fact we have a game in which we keep track of the points over several weeks and months. The winner (along with his wife) is the dinner guest of the loser (and his wife) and the choice of the restaurant is solely in the hands of winner and wife. This can be a little costly. So, winning is important. Fred and I felt that if we were to take time away from our spouses to play golf together, then a prudent decision about winning should involve wives. Great game. Great fun. Great way for all four of us to have a special meal a few times per year (hopefully paid for by the other fellow) to celebrate friendship and golf.

Here is the real story. Fred is so honest that we can play against one another and not even be on the golf course at the same time. I have no need to concern myself with his scorekeeping. He would never cheat me. If he tells me he deserves a few strokes from me, he gets them. He does not break the rules. His integrity is his greatest asset. We sometimes play together and other times we simply compare scores. It is our understanding that honesty and fair play are the foundation, not only of golf, but also of life.

Are there other people like Fred out there? Yes. Find them. Thank them. Treasure them. For it is the "Freds" of our society who will restore trust and rebuild the integrity of the marketplace.

Community is strengthened when individuals engage in supportive behaviors that contribute to the confidence and security of every participant. From the family to the factory, from the neighborhood to the nation, every transaction can build trust. The accumulation of these "unremembered acts" provides leaders with the opportunity to nurture an environment of trust and predictability. Such stability sustains community.

Step five is the act of bringing an integrity-centered leadership process into our society, which may be the only way to renew and revitalize the marketplace and restore confidence across the board. The following nine actions can help lead to the successful transmitting of values that renew and revitalize organizations:

1. Clarify core values by listening to leaders

2. Codify principles that translate into application

3. Communicate behaviors that sustain organizational effectiveness

4. Educate all stakeholders in principles of character

5. Support process extension from input for improvement

6. Measure content against mission and certify achievement

7. Monitor integration into culture alongside operational strategy

8. Recognize ongoing need to secure expanding commitment

9. Prepare for succession against backdrop of the integrity keystone, and anticipate beginning again at action #1: clarifying core values

Obviously, once leaders are willing to act on Step five, bringing the integrity-centered leadership process to their respective organizations, there is a need to assess progress against the Eight Attributes that create an atmosphere for effectiveness and productivity.

We know that the confidence of the American people in corporate leadership is low. The stain of scandal has undermined consumer trust and lowered stock prices. The ebb of confidence in leadership is even evident in the arena of government; in 2003 the people of California voted to recall the elected governor of that state. It is clear that the confidence of the people in their leaders is at a low point, if not an all-time low.

History, as always, can be a great teacher. A generation ago the United States was in a similar situation in relationship to the quality of its products. There grew a large national conversation about quality, arising out of the shock of U.S. workers who felt that the quality of the automobiles produced in Japan and Germany far outpaced those produced at home. The J.D. Power and Associates award for automotive consumer satisfaction, which first identified this problem, gained favor. Out of that great discussion of quality concerns were developed a variety of initiatives to improve quality. Motorola created, promoted and taught the six sigma quality process, and General Electric picked up the lead and carries that program initiative for the public today. Congress stood behind the Malcolm Baldridge National Quality Award, named for the late Secretary of Commerce who was highly regarded for improving efficiency and effectiveness within government. Today, quality is assumed, and most people would acknowledge their confidence in the quality of our nation's products.

A similar effort is required in the arena of integrity. We need a national conversation— at home, at work, in our communities, among our leaders, and in the body politic—about integrity-centered behavior. If every newspaper in our land joined in, if the radio and TV talk shows participated, and if our various monitoring institutions (e.g., the Securities and Exchange Commission and the Board of the New York Stock Exchange) demanded integrity-centered behavior, then the level of national focus and discussion would reach a critical mass. Indeed, behavior would change for the better. Within the free market system itself, we know from our experience with quality that if we demand integrity-centered behavior from our leaders, they will respond. We need a way to make integrity-centered behavior the great national conversation. If we design and build an integrity initiative in the proper way, it is bound to receive attention at a personal, community, regional and national level. Why? Because most people are decent, and that innate decency responds to integrity.

Every stakeholder must examine the values of those who would aspire to be leaders in every area of endeavor. Mediocrity can no longer be tolerated. White-collar crime ought to be attacked as strongly as robbery is today. Our local, state and national officials would provide leadership in the pursuit of truth, justice and the right path, instead of too often simply responding to the latest opinion poll. Integrity-centered behavior would become the reason to elect someone to public office. Confidence in our leaders would be restored.

We have a system of government that is responsive to the will of the people, over time, in a deliberate and measured way. The risk to our survival arises from a gradual deterioration in our values as a people; the forms of legislation that would become necessary to then regulate that behavior, and the virtual bondage that would result. We must follow the path of restoring integrity-centered behavior if we are to avoid the trap envisioned by Professor Alexander Tyler in 1778, and described in Chapter 1. We must remember his challenge to our system and become determined to avoid the pitfalls. His warning is worth repeating:

> A democracy cannot exist as a permanent form of government. It can only exist until the voters discover that they can vote themselves money from the public treasure. From that moment on the majority always votes for the candidates promising the most money from the public treasury, with the result that a democracy always collapses over loose fiscal policy followed by a dictatorship.
>
> The average age of the world's great civilizations has been two hundred years. These nations have progressed through the following sequence:
>
> > from bondage to spiritual faith,
> > from spiritual faith to great courage,
> > from courage to liberty,
> > from liberty to abundance,
> > from abundance to selfishness,
> > from selfishness to complacency
> > from complacency to apathy,
> > from apathy to dependency,
> > from dependency back to bondage.

Unless trust in leadership is restored soon, the dream of freedom and free markets may be beyond the reach of future generations. If integrity-centered behavior does not replace shortsighted greed and selfishness, then government officials will be forced into a position to pass even more laws that further stifle autonomy with over-regulation. These attempts to control misbehavior are guaranteed to frustrate legitimate creativity and smother freedom.

If we are to maintain freedom and free markets, integrity must be restored, beginning with the individual and family and extending all the way to those institutions upon which we depend. The building of an integrity-centered society occurs when trust exists between and among all stakeholders. When the Eight Attributes constitute the foundation for all transactions, confidence in leadership will have been restored so that all leaders—parents, educators, spiritual counselors, government employees of every kind, role models and leaders of the businesses community—behave in ways that nurture and inspire those around them.

1. CHARACTER: Consistency Between Word and Deed

2. HONESTY: Truthful Communication

3. OPENNESS: Operational Transparency

4. AUTHORITY: Employee Encouragement

5. PARTNERSHIP: Honor Obligations

6. PERFORMANCE: Accountability Throughout the Organization

7. CHARITY: Generous Community Stewardship

8. GRACIOUSNESS: Respect and Discipline

We know what once was good and could be good again. And we can make it happen. It begins one integrity-centered step at a time, by each individual. We make these commitments and take these actions on behalf of our children and grandchildren, as well as the grandchildren of our grandchildren. Because integrity matters.

*Integrity-centered leadership is the only reliable foundation
for long-term success!*
—Jim Bracher

About the Authors

James F. (Jim) Bracher created the **Bracher Center for Integrity in Leadership** in 2002 as an extension of his 33 years advising individuals and organizations. Those who have sought Jim's counsel include entrepreneurs, corporate executives and individuals addressing succession concerns. Jim's leadership development firm, Dimension Five Consultants, Inc., of which he is Founder and Chairman, is located in Monterey, California, and was established in 1980.

Prior to Dimension Five, Jim, an ordained clergyman, served 10 years as a chaplain, associate minister and senior pastor. His assignments were Saint Louis Country Day School in Ladue, Missouri; Second Congregational Church in Greenwich, Connecticut; First Congregational Church in Terre Haute, Indiana; and Community Church of the Monterey Peninsula in Carmel, California.

The motivation for the Bracher Center grew from suggestions of clients. They realized that Dimension Five was collecting data concerning effective and integrity-centered leadership that would enable leaders to gain insight into their own operational effectiveness as well as that of their organizations. Jim also saw a need for a Resources section on the Center's Website focused on learning, study and knowledge concerning the role of integrity in effective leadership. The Bracher Center shares insights that have been gained by Dimension Five in consultation with 8,000 leaders.

Jim's education includes a Bachelor of Arts, Elmhurst College; and a Master of Divinity, Eden Theological Seminary. He has continued his education at Whittier College, Hebrew Union University, Oxford University and the Hudson Institute.

His work has been featured on network television and in national newspapers and business journals. He is the originator of the "Talking with Leaders" symposia.

Jim's professional experience includes advisory councils and boards of directors. Along with his advisors and faculty at the Bracher Center, he restores integrity through insight.

Daniel E. (Dan) Halloran provides integrity-centered consulting with an emphasis on increasing international impact. He also directs the expansion of the Bracher Center for Integrity in Leadership. As a natural extension of his 40 years in business, he provides the Bracher Center with a multi-disciplinary approach derived from assignments in human resources, finance, sales and operations. Dan's global perspective has been refined through leadership he provided for Motorola to the countries and cultures of Greater Asia, Europe, the Middle East, Africa and the Americas.

Dan ended his 33-year Motorola, Inc. career as a Vice-President in 2001. Prior to joining the Bracher Center for Integrity in Leadership, Dan was responsible for the human resource delivery system for the Asia Pacific Region for four of the businesses of Motorola. He later directed the shared services functions supporting Motorola's 30,000 employees in the Asia Pacific Region.

Dan supported Motorola's Asia Pacific Region while residing in Seoul, Hong Kong and Singapore. Moving to London, Dan directed staffing functions across Europe, the Middle East and Africa. He has managed public seminars in human resources for the Australia Quality Council in Melbourne, Canberra and Sydney; on behalf of Motorola University in Kuala Lumpur and Singapore, and on behalf of the American Society of Training & Development in Phoenix, Arizona.

Dan served as a board member of Motorola Shanghai Paging Products Co., Inc., and on the Motorola Ethics Boards in China, Korea and Singapore. He was a guest lecturer at the European Institute of Business Management (INSEAD) and Harvard University on the Management of Expatriate Employees, as well as for the Industrial Relations Institute in Seoul and the Japan Council on Aging in Tokyo.

Dan earned his Bachelor of Arts at the University of Notre Dame and received his Masters in Business Administration from Arizona State University. Professional and community involvements have included serving on boards of civic, charitable and professional organizations.

Bracher Center for Integrity in Leadership

If you are interested in developing integrity in your business, capturing customers, motivating your workforce, and setting your organization apart, then turn to our consulting services and come away with a process to reignite the fire that drives integrity inside and beyond your enterprise.

VISION — Restore integrity through insight.
A world in which people do what they say, are forthright in their communications, and a handshake solidifies any promise.

MISSION — Provide integrity-centered leadership counsel.
Through our integrity-based services, we improve productivity for the investor, executive, team, culture, organization and the individual.

HISTORY and PURPOSE
When businesses fail in their values, they decay from the inside. In the late 1990's, values came to be viewed as expensive and conservative relics of the old economy. In the race to sell the latest and greatest product or service, the false promises of hollow values spoke too frequently to what we would not or could not do. As we begin the Twenty-first Century, the excesses of a few appear to have punished the whole of society, especially the economy. A world has been created where the prevailing structures promote the politics of convenience over the commitment of leadership. Too large a part of the business community enjoyed the excesses of luxury as it drifted from quick deals to devastating dishonesty. It should be common knowledge that free markets must regulate themselves or governments will.

Bracher Center for Integrity in Leadership
1400 Munras Avenue
Monterey, California 93940
Phone: (831) 373-5575
Fax: (831) 373-0994
E-mail: info@brachercenter.com
Website: www.brachercenter.com
Also: www.integritymatters.com

Index